The Genuin
Whole Food
Plant-Based Cookbook

Cleanse and Energize Your Body with a 3-Week Adventure in Pure Eating Sourced from Nature's Finest Offerings

Carolyn Constance

TABLE OF CONTENTS

Introduction

Welcome, dear reader, to a world where your plate is not just a dish but a canvas, and every meal is a brushstroke on the vibrant mural of your health. This book is more than just a collection of recipes; it's an invitation to embark on a gastronomic voyage that promises to be as delightful as it is nourishing. Here, we explore the timeless allure of whole food, plant-based eating—a tradition that has sustained civilizations, inspired poets, and, dare I say, made a few vegetables more popular at parties than some celebrities.

Imagine, for a moment, that your kitchen is a sanctuary, a place where the ordinary transforms into the extraordinary, where ingredients as humble as lentils and carrots are elevated to the status of culinary stars. With every recipe, you're not just preparing a meal, but engaging in a ritual that connects you to the earth, to cultures both ancient and modern, and to a philosophy of eating that prioritizes wellness in every bite. This isn't just about filling your stomach; it's about nourishing your soul.

As you journey through the pages of this book, envision yourself as both a connoisseur and a culinary explorer, discovering the lush landscapes of leafy greens, the robust villages of hearty grains, and the bustling cities of beans and legumes. Picture yourself strolling through a vibrant market, where the colors of fruits and vegetables are so vivid they almost sing. You're not just adopting a new diet but joining a global feast that has been in the making since the dawn of agriculture, one that's rich with the wisdom of generations who understood that the simplest foods often hold the most profound nourishment.

But fear not! You won't need a compass or hiking boots for this expedition—just a spoon, some curiosity, and perhaps an adventurous palate. This journey is accessible to all, from seasoned chefs to those who have only begun to explore their kitchen possibilities. Along the way, you'll learn to wield the mighty spatula not as a mere kitchen utensil but as a wand that transforms simple ingredients into spells of well-being and joy. The kitchen becomes your laboratory, where you experiment with flavors and textures, and discover that healthy eating doesn't have to be a chore—it can be a celebration.

Get ready to share a hearty laugh with those who have never found joy in a Brussels sprout, and to form bonds with fellow travelers united by a shared love for food that's as good for the soul as it is for the body. In these pages, you'll find more than just recipes—you'll find a community. A community that values not just what we eat, but how we eat it—mindfully, joyfully, and with a deep appreciation for the bounty that nature provides. Our journey is lined with feasts, festivity, and a fair amount of fiber—enough to keep us all in high spirits. The sense of community and shared love for healthy food will keep you connected and inspired throughout our culinary adventure.

So, tighten your apron, sharpen your knives, and let's turn the simple act of eating into a celebration of life. Every recipe is an opportunity to savor the present moment, to connect with loved ones, and to honor the ingredients that make it all possible. After all, every great meal begins with a warm welcome, and here, my friend, you are most warmly welcomed indeed. This book is not just a guide; it's a companion on your journey to health, happiness, and a life filled with delicious memories.

Let's begin this culinary adventure together, and may it fill more than just your stomach—may it fill your life with health, happiness, and a hefty dose of humor. Whether you're here to revolutionize your diet, to find new favorites, or simply to indulge in the joy of cooking, you've come to the right place. Welcome aboard, and let the feast begin!

Chapter 1: The Whole Food Plant-Based Revolution

The Origins and Philosophy of Whole Food Plant-Based Eating

Tracing the lineage of whole food, plant-based diets unveils a rich mosaic that blends ancient traditions with modern scientific insights. Throughout history, numerous cultures across the world have predominantly relied on plants for sustenance. This choice stemmed not only from agricultural practices but also from a profound recognition of the intrinsic benefits associated with plant-based foods. From the fertile stretches of the Nile Valley to the abundant gardens of the Aztecs, plants were not only esteemed for their availability but also for their medicinal qualities. Historical records and anthropological studies suggest that these societies encountered fewer chronic ailments compared to today's populations, highlighting the health advantages of diets laden with fruits, vegetables, grains, and legumes.

In contemporary times, the resurgence in whole food plant-based diets is more a renaissance than a novelty. Modern nutritional science provides a solid foundation that corroborates the extensive health benefits of plant-based eating. Experts in nutrition underscore its potential to mitigate the risk of major health issues such as heart disease, hypertension, and type 2 diabetes, alongside enhancing digestive health and promoting longevity. This scientific endorsement has elevated the plant-based diet from a simple nutritional choice to a comprehensive lifestyle that champions wellness and vitality.

Philosophically, the whole food plant-based diet goes beyond mere sustenance. It adopts a holistic view of health where food serves as medicine, not just as nourishment. This approach suggests that consuming whole, unprocessed foods aligns our bodies with their natural rhythms, fostering improved health outcomes. It encourages a reconnection with the sources of our food, promoting an awareness of the cultivation, preparation, and consumption processes. This appreciation not only deepens our connection to the environment but also supports sustainable farming practices, reducing our dependence on processed and industrially produced foods.

Adopting a whole food plant-based diet also signifies a commitment to ethical eating. It reflects a respect for life and natural systems, emphasizing the importance of nourishing oneself in a manner that harmonizes with the natural world and respects its cycles. This ethical dimension extends beyond personal health, influencing wider social values towards more sustainable and compassionate practices.

For many, choosing this diet aligns with values of compassion and non-violence, lessening the environmental impact associated with extensive animal farming and addressing the ethical concerns of animal welfare in food production. The shift is viewed not merely as a personal health choice but as an ethical stance that challenges conventional food systems, advocating for a regime that honors the planet and all its inhabitants.

Furthermore, the community surrounding whole food plant-based eating is dynamic and supportive, offering a sense of inclusion to those who join this path. Online platforms, local groups, and numerous publications support the transition, providing advice and shared experiences. This community aspect emphasizes the diet's philosophical roots in mindfulness and conscious consumption, resonating deeply in our fast-paced, often detached modern society.

Understanding the origins and deeper philosophy of whole food plant-based eating thus provides a compelling framework for those considering dietary changes. It invites individuals to engage in a practice that is both time-honored and critically relevant, merging health, ethics, and environmental stewardship in a way that promises to transform not only personal lives but also the broader food landscape. As we confront global health and ecological challenges, the principles of this diet offer not just nourishment but a route to restoration—both personal and planetary. The journey towards a whole food plant-based lifestyle is about rediscovering ancient truths and carving new paths to living, marking a revolution that is as transformative as it is enriching.

The Science Behind the Diet: Research and Results

The journey to understanding the benefits of a whole food plant-based diet often begins with curiosity and leads to discoveries that are both profound and transformative. Scientific research plays a crucial role in this exploration, offering insights that not only validate personal experiences but also reveal the extensive health benefits that this diet can provide. As we delve into the studies and findings, it becomes clear why so many health professionals and nutritionists are advocating for this lifestyle change.

Exploring the Impact on Chronic Diseases

The relationship between chronic diseases and diet is well-established, with a growing body of evidence underscoring how crucial dietary choices are in the prevention and management of conditions such as heart disease, type 2 diabetes, and certain types of cancer. A diet that prioritizes fruits, vegetables, whole grains, and legumes—the cornerstone of a whole food plant-based diet—plays a pivotal role in mitigating the risk and impact of these diseases.

Heart disease, for instance, is significantly influenced by dietary factors, particularly through mechanisms involving blood pressure and cholesterol levels. Plant-based diets are high in dietary fiber, antioxidants, and phytonutrients that collectively contribute to cardiovascular health. Fiber helps reduce blood cholesterol levels by binding to cholesterol in the digestive system and removing it from the body before it can circulate. Moreover, the natural low-fat content and absence of cholesterol in plant foods help maintain a healthier lipid profile.

In the realm of diabetes management, the high fiber content of a plant-based diet also proves beneficial. Fiber moderates blood glucose levels by slowing the absorption of sugar, improving overall blood sugar control. This can prevent spikes in blood glucose, which is critical in diabetes management. Furthermore, studies, such as those published in the *Diabetes Care* journal, have observed that diets rich in plant-based foods can improve insulin sensitivity and reduce inflammatory markers, both of which are crucial for managing diabetes.

The link between diet and certain types of cancer is also compelling. Diets rich in fruits and vegetables are linked to a reduced risk of cancer, especially cancers of the digestive system. This beneficial effect is often credited to the antioxidants and phytochemicals found in plants, which neutralize harmful carcinogens. Cruciferous vegetables like broccoli and Brussels sprouts are particularly noteworthy. They contain glucosinolates, which, when metabolized, form compounds known to impede the growth of cancer cells.

Furthermore, the alkaline nature of plant-based foods can influence the body's pH balance towards a more alkaline state, which some preliminary studies suggest may be less conducive to cancer growth compared to an acidic environment. Though this area of research is still evolving, the initial findings provide an interesting insight into how diet might influence cancer risk.

Beyond these specific diseases, the anti-inflammatory properties of many plant-based foods can play a broad role in disease prevention. Chronic inflammation is a known risk factor for many diseases, and the anti-inflammatory properties of foods like turmeric, ginger, berries, and greens can help reduce this risk.

The cumulative impact of these factors is profound. By adhering to a plant-based diet, individuals not only reduce the risk of chronic diseases but also enhance their overall health, leading to better long-term outcomes. The evidence from numerous studies consistently supports the notion that the foods we choose to eat have a direct and significant effect on our health trajectory. Thus, a plant-based diet transcends its role in disease prevention, establishing itself as a fundamental component for maintaining a vigorous and healthy lifestyle.

Nutritional Benefits and Body Systems

The rich nutritional profile of a whole food plant-based diet plays a central role in promoting health and preventing disease. This diet is abundant in dietary fiber, antioxidants, phytochemicals, and essential vitamins and minerals, each contributing uniquely to the maintenance and enhancement of bodily functions. The synergy of these nutrients supports various body systems in a holistic and effective manner.

Dietary Fiber: Beyond Digestive Health

While the role of dietary fiber in promoting digestive health is well-known, its benefits extend much further. Fiber helps stabilize blood sugar levels by slowing the absorption of sugar, which is particularly beneficial for preventing spikes after meals and managing long-term conditions such as diabetes. Additionally, fiber's ability to bind to cholesterol and facilitate its excretion from the body makes it a key player in cardiovascular health by helping to maintain lower cholesterol levels. Beyond these, fiber contributes significantly to weight management. By promoting satiety, or a feeling of fullness, it reduces overall calorie intake, which can help prevent obesity—a major risk factor for numerous health conditions including heart disease, diabetes, and joint problems.

Antioxidants and Phytochemicals: Cellular Protectors

Antioxidants are vital in defending against oxidative stress, a process that contributes to cellular damage and aging. Oxidative stress is associated with the onset of chronic diseases, including heart disease, Alzheimer's disease, and various cancers. The antioxidants present in plant-based foods such as berries, nuts, and green leafy vegetables work to neutralize free radicals, thereby shielding cells from potential damage. This not only supports the immune system but also helps maintain the integrity of cells and tissues across the body.

Phytochemicals, which are compounds produced by plants, also contribute to health and wellness. These substances, such as lycopene in tomatoes and resveratrol in grapes, have been studied for their potential to modulate inflammation, support heart health, and protect against cancer. Each plant food contains unique phytochemicals, which is why dietary diversity can be particularly beneficial, providing a range of these protective compounds.

Vitamins and Minerals: Essential for Bodily Functions

Vitamins and minerals are fundamental to a wide range of bodily processes. For instance, magnesium, abundant in leafy greens, nuts, and seeds, is essential for proper muscle and nerve function, maintaining a regular heart rhythm, and regulating blood pressure and blood sugar levels. Calcium, crucial for bone health, is readily available in fortified plant milks and dark leafy greens, making it possible to meet calcium needs without relying on dairy products. Iron, necessary for the production of red blood cells and the transport of oxygen throughout the body, can be sourced from plant-based foods like lentils and spinach. When consumed alongside Vitamin C-rich foods, such as fruits and vegetables, iron absorption is significantly enhanced, ensuring that a plant-based diet can effectively support these vital functions. This interaction showcases the importance of a varied diet to maximize nutrient uptake. The impact of a whole food plant-based diet on bodily systems is profound. By providing a rich array of macro and micronutrients, this diet supports the holistic functioning of the body, promoting not only the health of individual systems but also the efficient and harmonious operation of the body as a whole. This comprehensive nutritional support is why a plant-based diet is often associated with a lower risk of developing chronic diseases and is seen as a sustainable approach to long-term health and wellness.

Documented Outcomes from Lifestyle Switches

The transformative potential of adopting a whole food plant-based diet reaches beyond prevention to actually reversing certain conditions. Clinical trials, notably those led by Dr. Dean Ornish, showcase how coronary artery disease can be reversed through lifestyle changes centered around a plant-based diet. Participants in these studies not only witnessed reductions in arterial plaque but also enjoyed improved blood flow and less frequent chest pain. Accompanying these physical health benefits were notable reductions in cholesterol levels and blood pressure, enhancing overall cardiovascular health.

The improvements extend into emotional well-being and quality of life. Patients often report heightened vitality, clearer thinking, better sleep quality, and improved mood states. These benefits likely stem from a combination of enhanced physical health and the psychological uplift that comes from taking proactive control over one's health.

The impact on diabetes management is equally compelling. A plant-based diet, rich in fiber, helps improve weight management, reduce fat intake, and increase dietary fiber—all beneficial for controlling diabetes. This diet slows the absorption of sugar, helping to stabilize blood sugar levels and reduce the need for medications. In some cases, individuals have even experienced complete remission of type 2 diabetes, demonstrating significant improvements in insulin sensitivity and beta-cell function. Furthermore, the diet's effects on other metabolic conditions like high cholesterol and hypertension are profound. The removal of trans fats, reduced calorie intake, and elimination of processed foods contribute to these benefits, helping to optimize overall metabolism. This not only supports weight management but also reduces inflammation, providing relief from conditions such as arthritis and certain autoimmune diseases.

This compelling body of research underscores the power of diet and lifestyle changes not just in managing but in reversing chronic diseases. Adopting a whole food plant-based diet can fundamentally alter the health trajectory of individuals, offering a new paradigm in healthcare that emphasizes dietary and lifestyle transformation as core elements of disease treatment and optimal health.

Comprehensive View of Plant-Based Eating

The comprehensive body of research on whole food plant-based diets offers a vivid illustration of the profound effects this way of eating can have on our health. This perspective goes beyond merely eliminating animal products—it highlights the rich spectrum of nutrients that plants provide and the positive impacts they have on our cellular functions and overall vitality.

Every plant-based meal is packed with vitamins, minerals, fiber, and phytochemicals that work together to enhance our health. These nutrients play critical roles in everything from energy production and neural function to cellular repair and immune system regulation. The abundance of fiber in plant foods not only aids in digestion but also plays a crucial role in maintaining stable blood sugar levels and a healthy gut microbiome, which recent studies suggest can influence everything from mood to immunity.

Additionally, the natural antioxidants present in fruits, vegetables, nuts, and seeds play a key role in combating oxidative stress—a condition associated with chronic inflammation and numerous degenerative diseases. By regularly consuming these foods, we continually support our body's ability to fend off and recover from oxidative damage. Moreover, the plant-based diet's low saturated fat and high nutrient density contribute to cardiovascular health, reducing the risk of heart disease by lowering cholesterol and improving arterial health.

As we integrate this knowledge into our daily eating habits, it's essential to view each meal as an opportunity to positively impact our health. This approach encourages us not only to avoid harmful foods but to actively choose foods that can enhance our well-being. The evidence is clear that subtle changes in diet can lead to significant improvements in health and longevity, suggesting that our food choices can be as powerful as medicine in preventing and treating diseases.

The science behind a whole food plant-based diet not only guides us in making healthier choices but also reinforces the idea that these choices can lead to lasting improvements in our quality of life.

Your Journey Begins: Tips for a Smooth Transition

Embarking on a whole food plant-based lifestyle is more than a mere shift in diet—it's a transformation that can enhance your vitality and open up a new world of flavors. However, making this transition can seem daunting at first, especially if you're accustomed to a diet rich in processed foods and animal products. The key is to approach this change with a blend of patience, planning, and openness to learning. Here, we'll explore practical tips to set you on a path to success, ensuring that the transition is not only manageable but also enjoyable.

Setting Realistic Goals

Start with setting realistic, achievable goals. If the idea of overhauling your diet overnight feels overwhelming, begin by incorporating one plant-based meal a day. Whether it's a vibrant breakfast smoothie or a hearty vegetable stew for dinner, this single meal can become a powerful catalyst for change. Gradually incorporate more plant-based meals into your diet as you become more comfortable and confident in your selections. It's important to remember that this is not a race. The objective is to make lasting, sustainable changes that will benefit you for a lifetime, rather than simply a short-term experiment.

Finding Your 'Why'

Identifying your motivation—your 'why'—can significantly bolster your commitment. For some, the motivation may be improving personal health, such as reducing cholesterol or managing diabetes. For others, ethical concerns about animal welfare or environmental sustainability may drive the decision to adopt a plant-based diet. It's helpful to write down your personal reasons and revisit them whenever your commitment feels challenged. This reminder can reinforce your resolve and keep you focused on your long-term goals. This personal reminder of what you stand to gain can keep you focused and inspired on days when old habits seem hard to break.

Learning the Basics

Understanding the basics of nutrition can dispel common myths and uncertainties about plant-based eating. It's important to know where to get essential nutrients that are typically associated with animal products, such as protein, iron, and calcium. Legumes, nuts, seeds, whole grains, and leafy greens are just a few examples of plant-based foods rich in these nutrients. Equipping yourself with this knowledge can help you create balanced meals that support your health goals.

Exploring New Foods

One of the joys of adopting a whole food plant-based diet is the opportunity to explore a wide array of foods. Perhaps you've never tried quinoa, kale, or tempeh; now's your chance to explore these ingredients and discover new favorites. Explore local farmers' markets, join food co-ops, or take part in community-supported agriculture (CSA) programs to access fresh, seasonal produce. Experimenting with different flavors and recipes can make meal preparation an enjoyable and adventurous experience, transforming it from a routine task into something to look forward to.

Building a Supportive Community

Transitioning to a new diet is more rewarding and less challenging when you have support. Look for local groups, online communities, or forums where people share meal ideas, celebrate their wins, and offer encouragement during tough times. Connecting with others who are on a similar path can provide a sense of community and belonging, which is invaluable. These connections not only offer practical support but also enhance your emotional well-being as you navigate this change.

Planning Ahead

Meal planning is a crucial tool in maintaining a whole food plant-based diet. It helps you avoid the pitfall of reaching for convenient, less healthy options when you're hungry and unprepared. Spend some time each week planning your meals. This can involve batch cooking, preparing snacks, or simply writing a grocery list that aligns with your meal plans. Being prepared reduces stress and makes sticking to your goals much easier.

Celebrating Small Victories

Every step you take towards a whole food plant-based lifestyle is a victory that should be celebrated. Whether it's choosing a salad over fast food, cooking a new plant-based recipe, or simply learning something new about nutrition, acknowledge these wins. Celebrating these moments can boost your morale and motivate you to continue.

Being Patient and Kind to Yourself

Finally, be patient with yourself as you embark on this journey. Changing dietary habits is a major life adjustment, and it's normal to experience setbacks along the way. View these challenges not as failures, but as opportunities for learning and growth. Treat yourself with kindness, recognizing that progress takes time and perseverance. Maintain a compassionate mindset, and remember that each meal is a new chance to nourish your body and align with your values.

As you incorporate these tips into your daily life, remember that transitioning to a whole food plant-based lifestyle is not just about what you're giving up but also about what you're gaining: health, vitality, and a deeper connection to the world around you. With each plant-based meal, you're taking a step towards a more sustainable future for yourself and the planet. Embrace the journey with an open heart and a willing spirit, and let the wholesome bounty of the Earth support and sustain you.

Chapter 2: Essential Nutrients and How to Get Them

Key Vitamins and Minerals

When you embrace a whole food plant-based diet, understanding where your essential nutrients come from is not just helpful—it's crucial. This chapter is designed to demystify the nutrients you need and to assure you that a plant-based diet can indeed provide all the necessary elements for a healthy body. The key lies in knowing which foods to choose to meet your nutritional needs without compromising taste or variety.

Vitamins: A Closer Look

Vitamins are vital for energy production, immune function, and cell health, among other critical roles in the body. Vitamin B12, often highlighted in discussions about plant-based diets, is essential for nerve function and blood cell formation. Traditionally sourced from animal products, B12 can also be obtained from fortified foods like plant milks, some soy products, and breakfast cereals, or through a simple daily supplement. This ensures you're covering your bases without any dietary compromise.

Vitamin D, another critical nutrient, is known as the sunshine vitamin because the body can produce it when exposed to sunlight. However, depending on where you live, sunshine might not always be readily available. Fortified foods once again come to the rescue, along with supplements, to ensure adequate levels regardless of your sun exposure.

Then there's Vitamin C, which is abundant in a plant-based diet; its sources include citrus fruits, strawberries, bell peppers, and dark leafy greens. Not only does it serve as a powerful antioxidant, but it also enhances iron absorption, making it especially valuable for overall health.

Minerals: The Building Blocks

Minerals such as iron, calcium, and zinc play pivotal roles in bodily functions. Iron, which is crucial for transporting oxygen throughout the body, can be found in two forms: heme and non-heme. Plant-based diets offer non-heme iron, which is more effectively absorbed when paired with foods rich in vitamin C. Excellent sources of non-heme iron include lentils, chickpeas, beans, tofu, and quinoa, along with cashews and seeds.

Calcium is famed for its role in bone health but is also important for muscle function and nerve transmission. It's a myth that only dairy products can provide calcium. In fact, leafy greens like kale, bok choy, and broccoli, and fortified plant milks are excellent sources of this essential mineral.

Zinc is vital for metabolism, immune function, and repair of body cells. Eating a variety of zinc-rich foods like whole grains, tofu, tempeh, legumes, nuts, and seeds throughout the day can help meet your needs.

A Synergistic Approach to Nutrition

What's fascinating about eating a variety of whole, plant-based foods is that they often provide more than one nutrient. For instance, almonds offer not only healthy fats and protein but also calcium and iron. Similarly, chia seeds are a good source of omega-3 fatty acids as well as calcium and iron. This synergistic effect means that eating a well-rounded diet can naturally cover most of your nutritional bases.

Understanding these nutrient sources allows you to plan your meals not just with nutrition in mind, but also with joy. The colors, textures, and flavors of plant-based foods make each meal an adventure in taste and health. Plus, knowing you're nourishing your body with every bite adds a satisfying dimension to eating.

As we move forward in our plant-based journey, remember that every meal is an opportunity to feed not just the body, but also the soul. With each leafy green, each crunchy seed, and every vibrant fruit, you're building a foundation of health that is as robust as it is delicious. Let this knowledge empower you as you continue to explore the abundant world of plant-based nutrition. The road to health is not just paved with good intentions but also with informed food choices, each contributing to a thriving life.

Protein Sources and Requirements

Protein often takes center stage in discussions about nutrition, especially when transitioning to a plant-based diet. There's a common concern that plant-based foods can't provide sufficient protein, but this myth can be quickly dispelled with a better understanding of both protein requirements and the plethora of plant-based protein sources available.

Understanding Protein Needs

Protein is vital for the body, playing a key role in building and repairing tissues, producing enzymes and hormones, and supporting immune function. The required amount of protein can differ depending on factors such as age, sex, level of physical activity, and overall health. For most adults, the general recommendation is to consume a minimum amount of protein that is a percentage of their total daily calories; however, this requirement increases for those who are very active or trying to build muscle.

It's useful to know that our bodies are quite efficient at recycling protein. This means that while intake is important, our bodies can also reuse much of the protein from cells that are broken down during normal bodily processes. Hence, the total need for dietary protein might not be as high as one might initially think.

Plant-Based Proteins: A Closer Look

The realm of plant-based proteins is both diverse and plentiful. Legumes, grains, nuts, seeds, and even certain vegetables all make significant contributions to your daily protein intake. Here's a deeper dive into these sources:

- **Legumes:** Beans, lentils, chickpeas, and peas are powerhouses of protein, fiber, and other nutrients like iron and potassium. A cup of cooked lentils, for example, provides about 18 grams of protein, making it a substantial contributor to daily protein needs.
- **Grains:** While often overlooked as a protein source, grains like quinoa, amaranth, and buckwheat are actually quite rich in this macronutrient. Quinoa is especially notable because it contains all nine essential amino acids, making it a complete protein, a rarity in plant-based sources.
- **Nuts and Seeds:** Almonds, peanuts, sunflower seeds, and flaxseeds not only offer protein but also healthy fats, which are important for heart health and maintaining good cholesterol levels. They're perfect for snacking, adding to salads, or using in various recipes to boost protein content.

- **Vegetables:** While vegetables are not as protein-dense as legumes or nuts, some, like broccoli and spinach, do have respectable amounts of protein, especially considering their low calorie content. Integrating a variety of vegetables into meals ensures that you're not only getting protein but a broad spectrum of vitamins, minerals, and antioxidants as well.

Soy Products: A Versatile Protein Source

Tofu, tempeh, and edamame, all derived from soybeans, are excellent sources of plant-based protein. Tofu, in particular, is incredibly versatile, fitting seamlessly into a variety of dishes, from stir-fries to smoothies. It readily absorbs flavors, making it an easy way to enhance both the taste and protein content of your meals.

Combining Proteins: An Art and Science

One intriguing aspect of plant-based eating is the concept of protein combining. Earlier beliefs held that plant-based eaters needed to combine certain foods within a meal to achieve a complete protein profile. However, current understanding is more flexible, indicating that as long as you consume a diverse range of foods throughout the day, your body will naturally obtain all the essential amino acids it needs.

Meeting and Exceeding Protein Needs

For those new to plant-based diets, it might be surprising to learn that it's not only possible to meet protein requirements but also to exceed them without much effort. Including a variety of protein sources in meals ensures that not only are protein needs met, but meals remain interesting and flavorful. For instance, a breakfast smoothie with hemp seeds, a quinoa salad for lunch, and a lentil curry for dinner provide a rich array of proteins.

Listening to Your Body

Each body is unique, and it's important to listen to yours and adjust your diet according to how you feel. Some might find they thrive on higher protein intakes, especially if they're active, while others might need less. Keeping a food diary and noting how you feel can be a helpful way to fine-tune your protein intake. Embracing plant-based proteins not only meets dietary needs but also introduces you to a world of diverse flavors and textures that enrich your culinary experience. It's an exploration that proves both satisfying and beneficial, aligning with a lifestyle that's sustainable, healthful, and deeply rewarding. As you continue to discover the vast options available, let your meals be guided by both nutrition and the joy of trying new, delicious foods.

Balancing Macros for Optimal Health

When we discuss balancing macros—short for macronutrients, which include carbohydrates, proteins, and fats—it's like exploring the art of crafting a perfect meal that supports all aspects of our health. This isn't about strict rules or just mixing random ingredients; it's about understanding how these essential nutrients work in harmony to fuel our bodies. Each macronutrient plays a unique role, and getting the right balance can enhance energy levels, improve metabolic health, and contribute to overall well-being.

Understanding the Role of Each Macronutrient

- **Carbohydrates:** Often misjudged in the world of nutrition, especially with the rise of low-carb trends. However, in a whole food plant-based diet, carbohydrates are not just your main energy source; they are also packed with fiber, vitamins, and minerals. The key is to opt for complex carbohydrates, such as whole grains, legumes, and root vegetables, which provide steady energy without the blood sugar spikes linked to refined carbs.
- **Proteins:** Crucial for tissue building and repair, among other essential functions. A plant-based diet offers an abundance of protein sources, and the secret is to incorporate a variety of these into your meals to ensure you obtain all the essential amino acids. This variety not only fulfills your nutritional requirements but also keeps your meals exciting and full of flavor.
- **Fats:** Essential too, not just for energy but also for absorbing vitamins and supporting cell growth. Healthy fats, especially those from plant-based sources such as avocados, nuts, seeds, and olive oil, play a vital role in supporting heart health and maintaining brain function. Unlike saturated fats, which can harm heart health, these healthy fats provide a concentrated source of energy and help to keep you feeling full and satisfied after meals.

Finding the Right Balance

Balancing these macronutrients doesn't require a calculator at every meal but rather an awareness of your body's needs, which can vary based on age, activity level, and health goals. A great starting point is to fill half of your plate with non-starchy vegetables, allocate a quarter to complex carbohydrates, and reserve the remaining quarter for protein sources. Adding a small amount of healthy fat will round out the meal, ensuring you get a mix of what your body needs.

It's important to listen to your body and adjust your macronutrient intake based on how you feel. For instance, if you're regularly active, you might find that you need more carbohydrates for energy. Or, if you're focusing on muscle repair and growth, increasing your protein intake could be beneficial. This flexibility is one of the strengths of a plant-based diet—it can be adapted to meet various health needs and goals.

The Impact of Macros on Health

The impact of well-balanced macronutrients goes beyond just feeling good. Scientific studies show that diets rich in complex carbohydrates, adequate protein, and healthy fats can help manage and prevent chronic diseases such as type 2 diabetes, heart disease, and obesity. For example, the fiber found in complex carbohydrates helps regulate blood sugar levels and improves digestive health, while adequate protein intake supports the immune system and muscle maintenance.

Moreover, balancing macros can influence mood and cognitive function. Diets that are rich in a variety of plant foods provide antioxidants and phytochemicals that combat inflammation, which has been linked to mood disorders and cognitive decline. Healthy fats, particularly those rich in omega-3 fatty acids, are known to support brain health and may help stabilize mood.

Adapting to Life's Changes

As life changes, so too might your macro needs. From the busy middle-aged years where stress might dictate a need for more grounding complex carbs, to later years when protein intake becomes crucial to maintain muscle mass and bone health, adapting your diet to your life stage can have profound health benefits.

Chapter 3: The Healthiest and Most Nutritious Plant Foods

25 Everyday plant foods that are staples of a healthy diet

1. **Spinach**

   o *Description and Health Benefits:* Spinach is a powerhouse of nutrients, known for its high content of vitamins A, C, and K, as well as iron and folate. It supports eye health, reduces oxidative stress, and enhances immune function.

   o *Nutritional Details:* Rich in dietary fiber, calcium, and protein.

   o *Usage Suggestions:* Add fresh spinach to salads, smoothies, or sauté it as a side dish with garlic and olive oil.

2. **Broccoli**

   o *Description and Health Benefits:* Broccoli is celebrated for its cancer-preventing potential, thanks to its high levels of sulforaphane. It also boosts heart health and supports digestive wellness.

   o *Nutritional Details:* Contains vitamins C and K, fiber, and potassium.

   o *Usage Suggestions:* Steam or roast with a touch of seasoning, or chop and add to stir-fries and casseroles.

3. **Carrots**

   o *Description and Health Benefits:* Carrots are high in beta-carotene, which is converted into vitamin A in the body. This nutrient promotes good vision, skin health, and immune function.

   o *Nutritional Details:* Offers vitamins B6, K, potassium, and antioxidants.

   o *Usage Suggestions:* Snack on raw carrots, roast them with herbs, or blend into soups for a sweet flavor.

4. **Quinoa**

   o *Description and Health Benefits:* Quinoa is a complete protein source, providing all nine essential amino acids, making it particularly valuable in vegetarian and vegan diets.

   o *Nutritional Details:* High in fiber, iron, and magnesium.

   o *Usage Suggestions:* Use as a base for salads, substitute for rice in dishes, or mix into breakfast bowls.

5. **Sweet Potatoes**

- o *Description and Health Benefits:* Sweet potatoes are nutrient-dense root vegetables rich in vitamins A and C, manganese, and fiber. They help stabilize blood sugar levels and enhance beta-carotene intake.

- o *Nutritional Details:* Packed with fiber and potassium.

- o *Usage Suggestions:* Bake or boil sweet potatoes for a simple side, slice into fries, or mash with a touch of cinnamon and nutmeg.

6. **Almonds**

- o *Description and Health Benefits:* Almonds provide a valuable combination of healthy fats, protein, and vitamin E, supporting cholesterol levels, brain health, and cell protection from oxidative damage.

- o *Nutritional Details:* A good source of dietary fiber, calcium, and iron.

- o *Usage Suggestions:* Add chopped almonds to oatmeal or yogurt, use almond flour in baking, or incorporate into savory dishes for added crunch and flavor.

7. **Blueberries**

- o *Description and Health Benefits:* Blueberries are among the highest antioxidant-rich foods, improving brain function and reducing the risk of heart disease.

- o *Nutritional Details:* High in vitamins C and K, and manganese.

- o *Usage Suggestions:* Blend into smoothies, sprinkle over cereal, or incorporate into muffins.

8. **Kale**

- o *Description and Health Benefits:* Kale is a nutrient-dense food with powerful antioxidant properties, including vitamins A, C, and K. It supports heart health and detoxification.

- o *Nutritional Details:* Offers a significant amount of calcium and iron.

- o *Usage Suggestions:* Make kale chips, add to salads, or blend into green smoothies.

9. **Black Beans**

- o *Description and Health Benefits:* Black beans are an excellent source of protein and fiber, promoting heart health and aiding in digestion and blood sugar regulation.

- o *Nutritional Details:* Rich in protein, fiber, folate, and magnesium.

o   <u>Usage Suggestions:</u> Incorporate into veggie burgers, soups, or wraps for a filling meal.

10.   **Chia Seeds**

- *Description and Health Benefits:* Chia seeds are high in omega-3 fatty acids, fiber, and protein. They improve heart health and support digestive health.
- *Nutritional Details:* Loaded with antioxidants and minerals such as calcium, magnesium, and zinc.
- *Usage Suggestions:* Sprinkle on top of salads, stir into yogurt, or soak to make chia pudding.

11.   **Avocado**

- *Description and Health Benefits:* Avocado is high in monounsaturated fats, promoting heart health and reducing inflammation. It's also rich in vitamins E, K, and C.
- *Nutritional Details:* Provides fiber and potassium.
- *Usage Suggestions:* Use in guacamole, slice on toast, or add to smoothies for creaminess.

12.   **Lentils**

- *Description and Health Benefits:* Lentils are a fantastic source of protein, iron, and fiber. They help improve energy levels and support circulatory health.
- *Nutritional Details:* High in folate and manganese.
- *Usage Suggestions:* Add to stews, make into a salad, or use as a base for vegetarian patties.

13.   **Walnuts**

- *Description and Health Benefits:* Walnuts are rich in omega-3 fatty acids, essential for brain health, and help reduce heart disease risk.
- *Nutritional Details:* Contains copper, vitamin B6, and phosphorus.
- *Usage Suggestions:* Mix into baked goods, toss in salads, or have as a snack.

14.   **Beets**

- *Description and Health Benefits:* Beets are high in dietary nitrates, which have blood pressure-lowering effects. They also enhance athletic performance and boost brain health.
- *Nutritional Details:* Provides folate, manganese, and potassium.
- *Usage Suggestions:* Roast for a sweet side dish, juice for a health drink, or grate into salads.

15. **Oats**

- *Description and Health Benefits:* Oats are well-known for their heart health benefits, particularly in lowering cholesterol and stabilizing blood glucose levels.
- *Nutritional Details:* Excellent source of magnesium, zinc, and phosphorus.
- *Usage Suggestions:* Prepare as porridge, bake into cookies, or use in granola bars.

16. **Red Bell Peppers**

- *Description and Health Benefits:* Red bell peppers are loaded with vitamins A and C, supporting immune function and skin health.
- *Nutritional Details:* Also contains fiber, vitamin B6, and folate.
- *Usage Suggestions:* Stuff with quinoa and vegetables, add to stir-fries, or roast and blend into soups.

17. **Pumpkin Seeds**

- *Description and Health Benefits:* Pumpkin seeds are a good source of magnesium, zinc, and fatty acids, crucial for maintaining heart health and hormone balance.
- *Nutritional Details:* High in antioxidants and other beneficial nutrients.
- *Usage Suggestions:* Add to trail mix, salads, or eat roasted as a snack.

18. **Garlic**

- *Description and Health Benefits:* Garlic boosts immune function and has antibacterial and antiviral properties. It's also known to reduce blood pressure.
- *Nutritional Details:* Contains manganese, vitamin B6, and vitamin C.
- *Usage Suggestions:* Mince and add to sautéed vegetables, incorporate into salad dressings, or roast whole for a milder flavor.

19. **Tomatoes**

- *Description and Health Benefits:* Tomatoes are a versatile and nutrient-packed fruit, especially rich in lycopene, a powerful antioxidant known for reducing the risk of heart disease and certain types of cancer. In addition to lycopene, tomatoes provide vitamins C and K, potassium, and folate, all of which contribute to overall health, including immune support, bone health, and heart function.
- *Nutritional Details:* High in vitamin C, potassium, folate, and vitamin K.
- *Usage Suggestions:* Add to salads, sandwiches, or cook down into a heart-healthy sauce.

20. **Pomegranates**

- *Description and Health Benefits:* Pomegranates are celebrated for their exceptionally high levels of antioxidants, particularly punicalagins and anthocyanins, which help combat oxidative stress and may reduce the risk of chronic diseases such as heart disease and cancer. These antioxidants also have potent anti-inflammatory properties, which can help reduce inflammation throughout the body. Additionally, pomegranates are a good source of vitamins C and K, as well as dietary fiber, supporting immune function, bone health, and digestion.
- *Nutritional Details:* Rich in vitamin C, potassium, and fiber.
- *Usage Suggestions:* Add seeds to salads, use juice in dressings, or enjoy as a fresh snack.

21. **Ginger**

- *Description and Health Benefits:* Ginger has potent anti-inflammatory and antioxidant effects, helping with nausea and reducing muscle pain. It's also known for its ability to aid digestion and boost immune function.
- *Nutritional Details:* Contains gingerol, a substance with powerful medicinal properties.
- *Usage Suggestions:* Incorporate into teas, soups, or stir-fries.

22. **Cauliflower**

- *Description and Health Benefits:* Cauliflower is high in fiber and B-vitamins, providing antioxidants and phytonutrients that can protect against cancer. It also contains choline, essential for learning and memory.
- *Nutritional Details:* High in fiber, vitamin C, vitamin K, and choline.
- *Usage Suggestions:* Roast, mash, or use as a low-carb substitute in pizza crusts and rice dishes.

23. **Asparagus**

- *Description and Health Benefits:* Asparagus is a natural diuretic and is rich in vitamin K, which is essential for coagulation and bone health. It's also a good source of fiber, folate, and vitamins A, C, and E.
- *Nutritional Details:* Provides fiber, folate, and vitamins A, C, E, and K.
- *Usage Suggestions:* Grill, roast, or steam, and serve with a drizzle of olive oil and lemon.

24. **Mushrooms**

- *Description and Health Benefits:* Mushrooms are rich in selenium, potassium, and B vitamins, enhancing the immune system and adding great flavor to dishes. Some varieties also provide vitamin D, which is important for bone health.

- *Nutritional Details:* High in B vitamins, selenium, and potassium; some varieties contain vitamin D.
- *Usage Suggestions:* Sauté with garlic, add to stews, or stuff with a mixture of herbs and breadcrumbs.

25. **Green Tea**

- *Description and Health Benefits:* Green tea is high in antioxidants, particularly catechins, which help prevent cell damage and reduce the formation of free radicals in the body. It also supports weight management and cardiovascular health.
- *Nutritional Details:* Contains bioactive compounds that improve health, including catechins and caffeine.
- *Usage Suggestions:* Drink freshly brewed to maximize nutrient intake, or chill for a refreshing beverage.

1. **Lentils**

   - *Description and Health Benefits:* Lentils are a superb source of plant-based protein, ideal for enhancing muscle strength and aiding in recovery. They provide essential amino acids needed for growth and repair.
   - *Nutritional Details:* Contains 18 grams of protein per cup cooked, along with iron and fiber.
   - *Best Uses:* Incorporate into soups, stews, or salads. They also make excellent vegetarian burger patties or loaves.

2. **Chickpeas (Garbanzo Beans)**

   - *Description and Health Benefits:* Chickpeas are versatile legumes packed with protein, helping to support muscle maintenance and satiety. They are also rich in fiber and iron.
   - *Nutritional Details:* Offers 15 grams of protein per cup cooked.
   - *Best Uses:* Create homemade hummus, add to salads, or bake into crunchy snacks.

3. **Black Beans**

   - *Description and Health Benefits:* Known for their protein and fiber content, black beans support energy levels and digestive health.
   - *Nutritional Details:* Provides 15 grams of protein per cup cooked, plus potassium and magnesium.
   - *Best Uses:* Excellent in Mexican dishes, as a filling for tacos or burritos, or blended into dips.

4. **Quinoa**

   - *Description and Health Benefits:* Unlike other plant foods, quinoa is a complete protein with all nine necessary amino acids. It's also gluten-free and rich in minerals.
   - *Nutritional Details:* 8 grams of protein per cup cooked, including manganese and magnesium.
   - *Best Uses:* Use as a base for salads, stir into soups, or serve as a side dish with vegetables.

5. **Tofu**

- *Description and Health Benefits:* Tofu, made from soybean curds, is a staple protein in vegetarian diets known for its versatility and ability to absorb flavors.
- *Nutritional Details:* Contains about 10 grams of protein per half-cup serving, plus calcium and iron.
- *Best Uses:* Marinate and grill, scramble like eggs, or add to Asian dishes for a protein boost.

6. **Tempeh**

- *Description and Health Benefits:* Tempeh, a fermented soy delicacy, stands out by delivering a robust profile of protein and fiber, making it a powerhouse addition to a nutritious diet. Its fermentation process makes nutrients more digestible.
- *Nutritional Details:* 16 grams of protein per 3 ounces, rich in probiotics.
- *Best Uses:* Slice for sandwiches, crumble into stir-fries, or use as a meat substitute in recipes.

7. **Edamame**

- *Description and Health Benefits:* These young soybeans are protein-rich snacks or side dishes that provide essential amino acids and fiber.
- *Nutritional Details:* 17 grams of protein per cup cooked, high in vitamin K and folate.
- *Best Uses:* Serve steamed with a pinch of salt, add to salads, or blend into spreads.

8. **Almonds**

- *Description and Health Benefits:* Almonds have a high protein and healthy fat content, making them an ideal snack for energy and heart health.
- *Nutritional Details:* 6 grams of protein per ounce, plus vitamin E and magnesium.
- *Best Uses:* Snack on raw or roasted, chop into salads, or use almond flour in baking for a protein-rich alternative.

9. **Spirulina**

- *Description and Health Benefits:* This blue-green algae is a powerhouse of protein, with a high concentration of nutrients per gram than most vegetables.
- *Nutritional Details*: 8 grams of protein per 2 tablespoons, rich in B vitamins and copper.
- *Best Uses:* Mix into smoothies, sprinkle on salads, or stir into soups for a nutritional boost.

10.   **Peanuts**

- *Description and Health Benefits:* Peanuts offer more protein than any other nut, and they're a good source of heart-healthy fats.
- *Nutritional Details:* 7 grams of protein per ounce, high in niacin and manganese.
- *Best Uses:* Enjoy as peanut butter, add to granola, or snack on roasted peanuts.

11.   **Sunflower Seeds**

- *Description and Health Benefits*: These seeds are a good source of plant protein and healthy fats, beneficial for skin health and cell repair.
- *Nutritional Details:* 5.5 grams of protein per ounce, plus vitamin E and selenium.
- *Best Uses:* Sprinkle on salads, stir into yogurt, or bake into bread for extra texture and nutrients.

12.   **Chia Seeds**

- *Description and Health Benefits:* Chia seeds are not only high in protein but also in omega-3 fatty acids and fiber, making them excellent for heart and digestive health.
- *Nutritional Details:* 4.7 grams of protein per ounce, also rich in calcium and antioxidants.
- *Best Uses:* Make chia pudding, sprinkle on smoothie bowls, or add to muffins for a protein boost.

13.   **Flaxseeds**

- *Description and Health Benefits:* Flaxseeds are rich in protein and omega-3 fatty acids, which support heart health and reduce inflammation.

- *Nutritional Details:* 10 grams of protein per 3 tablespoons, also contains significant amounts of iron and zinc.

- *Best Uses:* Blend into smoothies, sprinkle over salads, or add to homemade granola bars for a protein enhancement.

14.   **Green Peas**

- *Description and Health Benefits:* Green peas are sometimes overlooked as a protein source, despite providing more protein than most vegetables. They are also rich in vitamins A, C, and K, contributing to overall health.
- *Nutritional Details:* 8 grams of protein per cup cooked, rich in vitamins A, C, and K.
- *Best Uses:* Add to soups, blend into a pesto, or mix into salads for a fresh, protein-rich addition.

15.   **Pumpkin Seeds**

- *Description and Health Benefits:* Pumpkin seeds, or pepitas, are a fantastic plant-based protein source, also providing magnesium, which is beneficial for heart health.
- *Nutritional Details:* 7 grams of protein per ounce, high in omega-3 fatty acids.
- *Best Uses:* Roast with spices for a snack, add to oatmeal or yogurt, or incorporate into energy bars.

16.   **Lima Beans**

- *Description and Health Benefits*: Lima beans are a potent protein source and are particularly high in fiber, which aids in digestion and promotes satiety.
- *Nutritional Details:* 15 grams of protein per cup cooked, also rich in potassium and iron.
- *Best Uses:* Include in stews, create bean salads, or mash into a creamy dip.

17.   **Seitan**

- *Description and Health Benefits:* Seitan, made from gluten, is known as "wheat meat" and provides a meat-like texture and flavor, making it popular in vegetarian cuisine.
- *Nutritional Details:* 21 grams of protein per 3-ounce serving.
- *Best Uses:* Use as a substitute in any dish that requires meat, such as stir-fries, sandwiches, and stews.

18.   **Buckwheat**

- *Description and Health Benefits:* Despite its name, buckwheat is gluten-free and loaded with protein and fiber. It's excellent for heart and metabolic health.
- *Nutritional Details:* 6 grams of protein per cup cooked, contains essential amino acids.
- *Best Uses:* Use in place of rice, make into porridge, or use buckwheat flour for gluten-free baking.

19.   **Adzuki Beans**

- *Description and Health Benefits:* Adzuki beans are a staple in Asian cuisine known for their sweet flavor and beneficial nutrients.
- *Nutritional Details:* 17 grams of protein per cup cooked, high in potassium and fiber.
- *Best Uses:* Ideal in Asian desserts, sprouted in salads, or mashed in savory dishes.

20. **Cashews**

   - *Description and Health Benefits:* Cashews provide a lower protein content compared to other nuts but are rich in iron, zinc, and beneficial fats.
   - *Nutritional Details:* 5 grams of protein per ounce, also high in magnesium and copper.
   - *Best Uses:* Use cashew butter in smoothies, sauces, or as a spread on toast.

21. **Amaranth**

   - *Description and Health Benefits:* Amaranth, often grouped with other pseudocereals like quinoa, offers a complete profile of essential amino acids, making it an outstanding source of plant-based protein. Rich in vitamins, minerals, and antioxidants, amaranth supports overall health and wellness.
   - *Nutritional Details:* 9 grams of protein per cup cooked, also rich in lysine and iron.
   - *Best Uses:* Add to soups for a protein boost, or use amaranth flour in gluten-free recipes.

22. **Teff**

   - *Description and Health Benefits*: Teff is a tiny grain packed with protein, calcium, and iron. It's ideal for maintaining bone strength and blood health.
   - *Nutritional Details:* 10 grams of protein per cup cooked.
   - *Best Uses:* Make into porridge or use teff flour for gluten-free baking.

23. **Mung Beans**

   - *Description and Health Benefits*: Mung beans are highly nutritious, providing protein, fiber, and antioxidants, and are known for their role in detoxification and lowering blood pressure.

   - *Nutritional Details:* 14 grams of protein per cup cooked.

   - *Best Uses:* Sprout for salads, make into mung bean pancakes, or use in curries.

24. **Pistachios**

   - *Description and Health Benefits:* Pistachios are a nutrient-dense nut that offers a balance of protein, healthy fats, and dietary fiber, making them a satisfying and nutritious snack. They are also rich in antioxidants, vitamins, and minerals like vitamin B6 and potassium, supporting heart health and digestion.
   - *Nutritional Details:* 6 grams of protein per ounce, also rich in vitamin B6 and thiamine.

- *Best Uses:* Add to salads, crush into crusts for meat or vegetable dishes, or snack on them raw.

25.   **Kidney Beans**

- *Description and Health Benefits:* Kidney beans are popular in chili and stews due to their high protein and fiber content, which aids in digestion and muscle growth.
- *Nutritional Details:* 13 grams of protein per cup cooked, also high in iron and magnesium.
- *Best Uses:* Use in chili recipes, salads, or make into a hearty bean dip.

1. Flaxseeds

- *Description:* Flaxseeds are a top source of ALA (alpha-linolenic acid), an essential omega-3 fatty acid that benefits heart health and helps reduce inflammation.
- *Nutritional Details:* Rich in omega-3 fatty acids, high in fiber, and a good source of lignans, which have antioxidant properties.
- *Usage:* Ground flaxseeds can be added to smoothies, oatmeal, or used as an egg substitute in vegan baking.

2. Chia Seeds

- *Description:* Chia seeds are rich in omega-3 fatty acids, fiber, and antioxidants, making them excellent for heart health and reducing inflammation. They also promote mental acuity and cognitive function.
- *Nutritional Details:* High in ALA omega-3s, fiber, and protein; excellent for digestive and cardiovascular health.
- *Usage:* Use in puddings, smoothies, or as a topping for yogurt and salads.

3. Walnuts

- *Description:* Walnuts are one of the richest plant-based sources of omega-3 fatty acids, vital for cognitive function and reducing inflammation. They also offer antioxidants that combat oxidative stress.
- *Nutritional Details:* High amounts of ALA omega-3 fatty acids and antioxidants.
- *Usage:* Ideal for snacking, adding to baked goods, or chopping into salads.

4. Hemp Seeds

- *Description:* Hemp seeds offer a balanced ratio of omega-3 to omega-6 fatty acids, supporting overall health and fighting inflammation. They are also a great source of GLA (gamma-linolenic acid) and protein.
- *Nutritional Details:* Rich in omega-3 and omega-6 fatty acids, GLA, and protein.
- *Usage:* Sprinkle on top of salads, blend into smoothies, or stir into yogurt.

5. Avocados

- *Description:* Avocados are high in oleic acid, a monounsaturated fat that helps reduce cholesterol levels and improve heart health. They are also loaded with fiber and potassium.
- *Nutritional Details:* High in monounsaturated fats, fiber, and potassium.

- *Usage:* Use in guacamole, spread on toast, or add to smoothies for creaminess without dairy.

6. **Almonds**

- *Description:* Almonds contain healthy monounsaturated fats and vitamin E, which help lower cholesterol and support overall health.
- *Nutritional Details:* High in monounsaturated fats, protein, magnesium, and vitamin E.
- *Usage:* Eat raw or roasted, use almond butter in smoothies, or almond meal in baking.

7. **Olive Oil**

- *Description:* Olive oil is rich in monounsaturated fats, particularly oleic acid, and phenolic antioxidants, which support cardiovascular health.
- *Nutritional Details:* High in monounsaturated fats and antioxidants.
- *Usage:* Ideal for dressings, drizzling over cooked dishes, or using in gentle sautéing.

8. **Sacha Inchi Nuts**

- *Description:* Known as the 'Inca peanut,' Sacha Inchi is high in omega-3, omega-6, and omega-9 fatty acids, promoting brain health and reducing inflammation.
- *Nutritional Details:* Exceptionally high in polyunsaturated fats and a good protein source.
- *Usage:* Eat as a snack, add to trail mixes, or enjoy their slightly nutty flavor.

9. **Pumpkin Seeds**

- *Description:* Pumpkin seeds are a good source of omega-6 and omega-3 fatty acids, as well as magnesium and zinc, supporting immune function and heart health.
- *Nutritional Details:* Offers healthy fats, antioxidants, and minerals.
- *Usage:* Roast as a snack, sprinkle on salads, or incorporate into bread.

10. **Sunflower Seeds**

- *Description:* Sunflower seeds provide polyunsaturated fats and vitamin E, which protect against heart disease and support immune function.
- *Nutritional Details:* High in vitamin E, selenium, and polyunsaturated fats.
- *Usage*: Add to salads, homemade granola, or bread recipes.

11. **Soybeans**

- *Description:* Soybeans are rich in omega-3 fatty acids, protein, and isoflavones, supporting cardiovascular and cognitive health.

- *Nutritional Details:* Rich in essential fatty acids, protein, and isoflavones.
- *Usage:* Enjoy in various forms such as edamame, tofu, or tempeh.

12. **Canola Oil**

- *Description:* Canola oil is known for its balance of omega-3 and omega-6 fatty acids and its low saturated fat content, making it heart-healthy.
- *Nutritional Details:* Low in saturated fat, high in monounsaturated and polyunsaturated fats.
- *Usage:* Ideal for cooking, baking, and dressings due to its mild flavor and high smoke point.

13. **Seaweed**

- *Description:* Seaweed is unique among plant-based foods for its content of EPA, an omega-3 fatty acid more commonly found in fish, as well as iodine, which is essential for thyroid health.
- *Nutritional Details:* Rich in EPA omega-3 fatty acids, iodine, and fiber.
- *Usage:* Include in sushi rolls, add to soups, or use as a salad ingredient.

14. **Mustard Oil**

- *Description:* Mustard oil is rich in ALA omega-3 fatty acids and erucic acid, contributing to its strong flavor and potential heart health benefits.
- *Nutritional Details:* Contains high levels of erucic acid and alpha-linolenic acid.
- *Usage:* Common in Indian and Bangladeshi cooking for frying or pickling.

15. **Macadamia Nuts**

- *Description:* Macadamia nuts are rich in monounsaturated fats and low in omega-6 fatty acids, reducing inflammation and supporting heart health.
- *Nutritional Details:* High in monounsaturated fats and low in omega-6 fatty acids.
- *Usage:* Enjoy raw or baked into desserts for a rich, buttery flavor.

16. **Pecans**

- *Description:* Pecans are loaded with antioxidants and healthy fats, promoting lower LDL cholesterol levels and supporting heart health.
- *Nutritional Details:* Rich in monounsaturated and polyunsaturated fatty acids, vitamin E, and fiber.
- *Usage:* Add to pies, salads, or enjoy as a snack.

17. **Pine Nuts**

- *Description:* Pine nuts contain pinolenic acid, which helps curb appetite, along with healthy monounsaturated fats, iron, and magnesium.
- *Nutritional Details:* High in iron, magnesium, and healthy fats.
- *Usage:* Ideal for making pesto, adding to salads, or as a topping on pasta.

18. **Hazelnuts**

- *Description:* Hazelnuts support cardiovascular health with their vitamin E content and healthy fats, and they are high in folate for cell function and growth.
- *Nutritional Details:* Provides monounsaturated fats, vitamin E, and antioxidants.
- *Usage:* Great in baked goods, crushed in salads, or ground into nut butter.

19. **Brazil Nuts**

- *Description:* Brazil nuts are rich in selenium, which supports thyroid function, along with unsaturated fats that prevent cellular damage.
- *Nutritional Details:* High in selenium and omega-6 fatty acids.
- *Usage:* Eat a few Brazil nuts a day for selenium; also great chopped in desserts or cereals.

20. **Cashews**

- *Description:* Cashews are lower in fat but rich in iron, zinc, and monounsaturated fats, supporting immune and mental health.
- *Nutritional Details:* Good source of magnesium, zinc, and healthy fats.
- *Usage:* Use in cashew milk, vegan cheeses, or as a creamy base for sauces.

21. **Olives**

- *Description:* Olives are rich in monounsaturated fats, which reduce heart disease risk, and they are also a good source of vitamin E and antioxidants.
- *Nutritional Details:* Rich in monounsaturated fats, vitamin E, and antioxidants.
- *Usage:* Add to Mediterranean dishes, tapenades, or enjoy as a healthy snack.

22. **Pistachios**

- *Description:* Pistachios are beneficial for weight management and heart health due to their high protein and healthy fat content.
- *Nutritional Details:* Contains more potassium and vitamin K per serving compared to other nuts.

- *Usage:* A great addition to salads, baked goods, or as a snack on their own.

23. **Coconut Oil**

- *Description:* Coconut oil is recognized for its medium-chain triglycerides (MCTs), which are metabolized differently than other fats and provide a rapid energy source, potentially aiding in weight management.
- *Nutritional Details:* Rich in saturated fats, particularly lauric acid, which can improve cholesterol levels and heart health.
- *Usage:* Versatile in both cooking and baking, it can be used to sauté vegetables, as a butter substitute, or even in coffee.

24. **Tahini**

- *Description:* Made from ground sesame seeds, tahini is high in both monounsaturated and polyunsaturated fatty acids, supporting heart health.
- *Nutritional Details:* Provides healthy fats, calcium, iron, and some protein.
- *Usage:* Commonly used in Middle Eastern dishes like hummus and baba ghanoush or as a base for dressings and sauces.

25. **Soybeans**

- *Description:* Soybeans are an excellent source of omega-3 fatty acids, vital for cardiovascular and cognitive health. They are also rich in protein and isoflavones, supporting overall health.
- *Nutritional Details:* Rich in essential fatty acids, protein, and isoflavones.
- *Usage:* Soybeans can be enjoyed in various forms, including edamame, tofu, and tempeh.

1. Blueberries

- *Description and Health Benefits:* Blueberries are often hailed as a superfood due to their high levels of antioxidants like anthocyanins, linked to reduced inflammation and cancer prevention.
- *Nutritional Details:* Rich in vitamins C and K and manganese.
- *Usage Tips:* Toss them in smoothies, sprinkle on oatmeal, or enjoy them fresh for a nutritious snack.

2. Kale

- *Description and Health Benefits*: This leafy green is loaded with vitamins and cancer-fighting antioxidants such as quercetin and kaempferol.
- *Nutritional Details:* High in vitamins A, C, K, and several B vitamins.
- *Usage Tips:* Add to salads, blend into smoothies, or bake into chips for a crunchy treat.

3. Spinach

- *Description and Health Benefits:* Spinach is packed with antioxidants like lutein and zeaxanthin, which are beneficial for eye health.
- *Nutritional Details:* Offers iron, folate, and vitamins A and C.
- *Usage Tips:* Mix into pasta dishes, sauté with garlic for a healthy side, or use as a base for salads.

4. Strawberries

- *Description and Health Benefits:* These berries are rich in vitamin C and key antioxidants that contribute to heart health and skin vitality.
- *Nutritional Details:* Abundant in vitamin C and manganese.
- *Usage Tips:* Perfect in desserts, cereals, or dipped in dark chocolate for an indulgent yet healthy treat.

5. Artichokes

- *Description and Health Benefits:* Artichokes are high in the antioxidant chlorogenic acid, which has potent liver health benefits.
- *Nutritional Details:* Contains fiber, vitamin C, and magnesium.
- *Usage Tips:* Boil or steam and serve with a dip, or incorporate into Mediterranean dishes.

6. Red Cabbage

- *Description and Health Benefits:* This vegetable offers anthocyanins, the same antioxidants found in blueberries, and is effective in reducing inflammation.
- *Nutritional Details:* Loaded with vitamins A, C, and K.
- *Usage Tips:* Great in slaws or fermented to make sauerkraut.

7. **Beans**

- *Description and Health Benefits:* Beans are not only a great protein source but also contain antioxidant compounds like isoflavones and phytosterols that enhance longevity.
- *Nutritional Details:* High in protein, fiber, iron, and potassium.
- *Usage Tips:* Ideal in chili, salads, or as a hearty soup base.

8. **Beets**

- *Description and Health Benefits:* Beets are a fantastic source of betalains, which have been studied for their cancer-fighting properties.
- *Nutritional Details:* Provides folate, iron, and manganese.
- *Usage Tips:* Roast to bring out their sweetness, or juice them for a nutrient-packed drink.

9. **Pecans**

- *Description and Health Benefits:* Pecans are filled with antioxidants that are beneficial for heart health and for lowering cholesterol levels.
- *Nutritional Details:* Rich in vitamin E and zinc.
- *Usage Tips:* Add to salads, desserts, or eat raw to enjoy their crunchy texture.

10. **Oranges**

- *Description and Health Benefits:* Oranges are celebrated for their high vitamin C content and powerful antioxidants like hesperidin and naringenin, which contribute to overall health.
- *Nutritional Details:* Excellent source of vitamin C and fiber.
- *Usage Tips:* Freshly squeezed juice, zest in baking, or segments in fruit salads.

11. **Dark Chocolate**

- *Description and Health Benefits:* High in flavonoids, particularly catechins, which boost heart health and can increase brain function.

- *Nutritional Details:* Also provides iron, magnesium, and copper.

- *Usage Tips:* Opt for varieties that contain at least 70% cocoa to maximize benefits.

12. **Carrots**

- *Description and Health Benefits:* Carrots are rich in beta-carotene, an antioxidant that the body converts into vitamin A, which is good for your eyes.
- *Nutritional Details:* High in vitamin A and fiber.
- *Usage Tips:* Snack on raw, juice them, or roast with herbs.

13. **Walnuts**

- *Description and Health Benefits:* Walnuts are a good source of healthy fats and contain ellagic acid, an antioxidant that helps reduce oxidative stress.
- *Nutritional Details:* Good source of alpha-linolenic acid (ALA), a plant-based omega-3.
- *Usage Tips:* Blend into nut butter, add to baked goods, or sprinkle over yogurt.

14. **Green Tea**

- *Description and Health Benefits:* Packed with catechins like EGCG, green tea is renowned for its ability to enhance brain health and lower cancer risk.
- *Nutritional Details:* Rich in polyphenolic compounds and minimal calories.
- *Usage Tips:* Drink freshly brewed to maximize the antioxidants, or cool down with an iced version.

15. **Raspberries**

- *Description and Health Benefits:* Raspberries offer quercetin and ellagic acid, antioxidants known for their anti-inflammatory and cancer-preventing properties.
- *Nutritional Details:* Also high in fiber and vitamins C and K.
- *Usage Tips:* Perfect in smoothies, desserts, or as a fresh snack.

16. **Plums**

- *Description and Health Benefits:* Plums contain unique antioxidants called chlorogenic acids, which can help lower anxiety.
- *Nutritional Details:* Also a good source of vitamins A and C.
- *Usage Tips:* Delicious fresh, or dried as prunes for a concentrated source.

17. **Blackberries**

- *Description and Health Benefits:* Blackberries are among the highest in antioxidants among all fruits, offering significant amounts of bioflavonoids and vitamins C and K.
- *Nutritional Details:* High in fiber and vitamin K.
- *Usage Tips:* Blend into smoothies, use in pies, or simply enjoy fresh.

18. **Kidney Beans**

- *Description and Health Benefits:* These beans are rich in protein and contain anthocyanins, an antioxidant compound that reduces inflammation and improves brain function.
- *Nutritional Details:* Great source of iron and manganese.
- *Usage Tips:* Add to stews, salads, or make into a hearty bean dip.

19. **Red Grapes**

- *Description and Health Benefits*: Red grapes are famous for resveratrol, a polyphenol that has been linked to a lower risk of heart disease and longevity.
- *Nutritional Details:* Contains vitamins C and K.
- *Usage Tips:* Freeze for a refreshing snack, add to salads, or enjoy in a glass of red wine.

20. **Pomegranates**

- *Description and Health Benefits:* Pomegranates are renowned for their impressive antioxidant content, which helps mitigate inflammation and offers protective benefits against heart disease and cancer.
- *Nutritional Details:* Rich in vitamin C, potassium, and fiber.
- *Usage Tips:* Use the seeds in salads, juices, or sprinkle over desserts.

21. **Tomatoes**

- *Description and Health Benefits:* Tomatoes are a vital dietary source of lycopene, an antioxidant associated with numerous health advantages, such as lowering the risk of heart disease and cancer.
- *Nutritional Details:* High in vitamins C and K and potassium.
- *Usage Tips:* Add to sandwiches, salads, or cook down into a sauce.

22. **Red Onions**

- *Description and Health Benefits:* Red onions are high in quercetin, an antioxidant that can fight inflammation and boost immunity.
- *Nutritional Details:* Also sources of vitamin C and B vitamins.
- *Usage Tips:* Use raw in salads, or caramelize to enhance their natural sweetness.

23. **Cranberries**

- *Description and Health Benefits:* Cranberries are packed with antioxidants that help prevent urinary infections and improve cardiovascular health.
- *Nutritional Details:* Good source of vitamin C and E.
- *Usage Tips:* Make into a sauce, add to baked goods, or drink as juice.

24. **Asparagus**

- *Description and Health Benefits:* Asparagus is loaded with beta-carotene, lutein, and zeaxanthin, antioxidants that support healthy vision and cellular health.
- *Nutritional Details:* Also provides fiber, folate, and vitamins A, C, and K.
- *Usage Tips:* Grill, roast, or steam for a delicious side dish.

25.   **Parsley**

- *Description and Health Benefits:* Often used as a garnish, parsley is a nutritional powerhouse with high levels of flavonoids, vitamin C, and vitamin K.
- *Nutritional Details:* Excellent source of antioxidants and essential oils that reduce inflammation.
- *Usage Tips:* Chop finely into dishes for a fresh flavor, or blend into a green smoothie.

Fiber-Focused Foods

1. Chia Seeds

- *Description:* Chia seeds are incredibly fiber-rich, aiding in digestion, maintaining satiety, and regulating blood sugar levels.
- *Nutritional Details:* Around 10 grams of fiber per ounce.
- *Usage Tips:* Sprinkle on yogurt, blend into smoothies, or soak to make chia pudding for a fiber boost.

2. Flaxseeds

- *Description:* High in both soluble and insoluble fiber, flaxseeds help with digestive health by promoting regular bowel movements and lowering cholesterol.
- *Nutritional Details:* Approximately 2.8 grams of fiber per tablespoon.
- *Usage Tips:* Grind and add to bread, muffins, or smoothies to enhance fiber content without altering flavor much.

3. Lentils

- *Description:* Lentils are rich in protein and high in fiber, aiding in digestive health and stabilizing blood sugar levels.
- *Nutritional Details:* About 15.6 grams of fiber per cup cooked.
- *Usage Tips:* Incorporate into soups, stews, or salads to significantly increase daily fiber intake.

4. Black Beans

- *Description:* Black beans are an excellent source of fiber, supporting the digestive tract and helping prevent blood sugar spikes after meals.
- *Nutritional Details:* Roughly 15 grams of fiber per cup cooked.
- *Usage Tips:* Perfect for adding to Mexican dishes, soups, or making hearty black bean burgers.

5. Avocados

- *Description:* Avocados are not only rich in healthy fats but also high in fiber, aiding in digestion and promoting satiety.
- *Nutritional Details:* About 10 grams of fiber per cup.
- *Usage Tips:* Use in guacamole, on toast, or as a fat substitute in baking to boost fiber content.

6. Oats

- *Description:* Oats are rich in beta-glucan, a soluble fiber known for its ability to lower cholesterol and protect against heart disease.
- *Nutritional Details:* Approximately 4 grams of fiber per cup cooked.
- *Usage Tips:* Start the day with a bowl of oatmeal, or use oats in baking to increase fiber intake.

7. Peas

- *Description:* Green peas are abundant in fiber, supporting digestive health and promoting a sense of fullness.
- *Nutritional Details:* About 9 grams of fiber per cup cooked.
- *Usage Tips:* Add to salads, soups, or blend into a creamy pea soup for a fiber-rich meal.

8. Brussels Sprouts

- *Description:* Often referred to as mini cabbages, Brussels sprouts are loaded with fiber and antioxidants, excellent for digestion and cellular health.
- *Nutritional Details:* 4 grams of fiber per cup cooked.
- *Usage Tips:* Roast with olive oil and sea salt for a delicious side dish rich in fiber.

9. Raspberries

- *Description:* Raspberries are among the highest-fiber fruits, aiding in regulating the digestive system and reducing the risk of chronic diseases.
- *Nutritional Details:* 8 grams of fiber per cup.
- *Usage Tips:* Add to cereals, desserts, or blend into smoothies for a sweet, fibrous addition.

10. Pears

- *Description:* With both soluble and insoluble fiber, pears improve digestive health and support weight management.
- *Nutritional Details:* About 6 grams of fiber per medium pear.
- *Usage Tips:* Eat fresh or bake into desserts for a fibrous, nutritious snack.

11. Artichokes

- *Description:* Artichokes are high in fiber, benefiting heart health by helping to lower cholesterol levels and stabilize blood sugar.
- **Nutritional Details:** 10 grams of fiber per artichoke.
- *Usage Tips:* Boil or grill and serve with a dip, or incorporate into pasta dishes.

12. Barley

- *Description:* Barley is a whole grain rich in vitamins, minerals, and fiber, enhancing digestion and offering cardiovascular benefits.
- *Nutritional Details:* 6 grams of fiber per cup cooked.
- *Usage Tips:* Use in soups, stews, or as a wholesome rice alternative.

13. **Almonds**

- *Description:* Almonds are beneficial for heart health and weight management due to their fiber and healthy fat content.
- *Nutritional Details:* 3.5 grams of fiber per ounce.
- *Usage Tips:* Snack on raw or roasted, add to salads, or use almond flour in baking.

14. **Whole Wheat Pasta**

- *Description:* Switching to whole wheat pasta can significantly increase your fiber intake, supporting digestive health and providing a slower release of energy.
- *Nutritional Details:* About 6 grams of fiber per cooked cup.
- *Usage Tips:* Pair with nutrient-rich sauces and vegetables for a balanced, fibrous meal.

15. **Broccoli**

- *Description:* Broccoli is rich in fiber and supports digestive health while providing protection against certain cancers.
- *Nutritional Details:* 5 grams of fiber per cup cooked.
- *Usage Tips:* Steam, stir-fry, or include in casseroles to maintain its nutritional integrity.

16. **Sweet Potatoes**

- *Description:* Sweet potatoes, especially when consumed with their skin, are a delicious source of dietary fiber, offering an abundance of vitamins and minerals.
- *Nutritional Details:* 4 grams of fiber per medium sweet potato.
- *Usage Tips:* Bake, mash, or turn into fries or chips for a versatile, fibrous addition to meals.

17. **Apples**

- *Description:* Apples offer soluble fiber to help control blood sugar levels and insoluble fiber to support digestion.
- *Nutritional Details:* 4 grams of fiber per medium apple.
- *Usage Tips:* Eat raw, bake into desserts, or add to salads for a sweet, crunchy texture.

18. **Carrots**

- *Description:* Carrots provide a healthy dose of fiber, aiding in digestion and lowering cholesterol.
- *Nutritional Details:* About 3.6 grams of fiber per cup.
- *Usage Tips:* Enjoy raw as snacks, roast with honey, or add to soups.

19. **Beets**

- *Description:* Beets are vibrant and flavorful, with fiber that supports liver and heart health.
- *Nutritional Details:* 3.8 grams of fiber per cup cooked.
- *Usage Tips:* Roast for salads, blend into smoothies, or pickle for extra flavor.

20. **Collard Greens**

- *Description:* Collard greens provide soluble fiber that helps lower cholesterol and maintain healthy digestion.
- *Nutritional Details:* 5 grams of fiber per cup cooked.
- *Usage Tips:* Sauté as a side, add to soups, or use as a wrap for a low-carb option.

21. **Bulgur Wheat**

- *Description:* Bulgur wheat is a whole grain that provides fiber, aiding in digestion and promoting fullness.
- *Nutritional Details:* 8 grams of fiber per cup cooked.
- *Usage Tips:* Use in tabbouleh, pilafs, or as a base in grain bowls for a hearty meal.

22. **Navy Beans**

- *Description:* Navy beans are very high in fiber, improving cholesterol levels and supporting digestive health.
- *Nutritional Details:* 19 grams of fiber per cup cooked.
- *Usage Tips:* Great in stews, soups, and salads, or pureed into a creamy spread.

23. **Pumpkin**

- *Description:* Pumpkin is high in fiber and low in calories, making it excellent for digestion and maintaining a healthy weight.
- *Nutritional Details:* 3 grams of fiber per cup cooked.
- *Usage Tips:* Incorporate into soups, pies, and smoothies, or roast as a side dish.

24. **Cauliflower**

- *Description:* Cauliflower offers a good amount of fiber, which aids in digestion and reduces inflammation.
- *Nutritional Details:* 3 grams of fiber per cup cooked.
- *Usage Tips:* Roast with spices, blend into soups, or use as a low-carb rice alternative.

25. **Kiwifruit**

- *Description:* Kiwifruit is delicious and a fantastic source of fiber, aiding digestion and providing vitamin C.

o   *Nutritional Details:* 2 grams of fiber per medium fruit.

o   *Usage Tips:* Eat fresh, add to fruit salads, or blend into smoothies for a nutritious snack.

DOWNLOAD YOUR EXCLUSIVE BONUS

Plant-Based Recipes and Culinary Traditions from Around the World

Thank you so much for purchasing my book and taking the time to download the bonus content!

I hope you found it valuable and enjoyable.

Your feedback means the world to me, and if you have a moment, I'd greatly appreciate it if you could leave a review.

Your thoughts help others discover the book and continue to support my work.

Thank you again for your support!

Chapter 4: Meal Planning and Preparation Tips

Grocery Shopping for Whole Food Plant-Based Diet

Embarking on a whole food plant-based diet begins where your food journey typically starts: the grocery store. This section will guide you through the process of shopping effectively to support your plant-based diet, helping you to select the freshest ingredients, stay within budget, and enjoy a variety of nutritious and delicious meals. Navigating the grocery store with a plant-based lens is an exciting opportunity to rediscover the abundance of natural foods available. Start by making the produce section your new best friend. Here, colors are vibrant, and the options are plentiful. For a well-rounded diet, it's important to include a diverse array of fruits and vegetables. This ensures you receive a comprehensive mix of vitamins, minerals, and antioxidants, essential for optimal health. Leafy greens like spinach, kale, and Swiss chard are staples for their nutrient density, while brightly colored vegetables like bell peppers, carrots, and beets add visual appeal and nutritional value to any dish. Whole grains are another cornerstone of a plant-based diet. When grocery shopping, prioritize whole, unprocessed grains such as quinoa, brown rice, barley, and oats. These grains are not only rich in essential nutrients like B vitamins and minerals but also enhance satiety and help stabilize blood sugar levels.

Legumes are an excellent choice for plant-based protein. Keep your pantry stocked with various beans, lentils, and chickpeas. These staples are budget-friendly and incredibly versatile, perfect for enriching soups, stews, and salads with both fiber and protein to keep you feeling full longer.

Don't forget about nuts and seeds. Almonds, walnuts, chia seeds, and flaxseeds provide healthy fats and add a delightful crunch to your meals. They're excellent for snacking or enhancing dishes with added texture and nutrients. When selecting nuts and seeds, choose raw or dry-roasted options without additional salt or flavorings to maximize health benefits. When it comes to healthier fats, don't overlook the importance of avocados, olives, and coconuts, which provide essential fatty acids and can enhance the flavor profile of your meals. Look for cold-pressed oils like olive or avocado oil for cooking and dressings. As you shop, it's crucial to read labels carefully. Even foods that seem like they should be plant-based can contain hidden animal products or unwanted additives. Check ingredients lists for items like gelatin, whey, and casein, which are animal-derived, and opt for products that are marked as vegan if you want to avoid these ingredients entirely. Another helpful tip is to plan your grocery trips based on what you already have at home. This can prevent overbuying and food waste. Make a list of what you need for the week's meals, and try to stick to it. This not only helps keep your shopping focused but also can help manage your food budget. Consider, too, the environmental impact of your food choices. Whenever possible, opt for local and seasonal produce to minimize your carbon footprint and support community farmers. Such choices often yield fresher, more flavorful fruits and vegetables. Additionally, using reusable produce bags and shopping bags during your grocery trips is a simple yet effective way to help reduce plastic waste, making a positive environmental impact with each visit to the market.

The journey through the grocery store is an integral part of your plant-based lifestyle. Each choice you make can contribute to a healthier body and a healthier planet. Embrace the diversity of foods available, and enjoy the process of planning and preparing meals that are not only good for you but also good for the environment. As you continue to explore the world of plant-based eating, let your grocery cart reflect your commitment to nourishing yourself and the planet sustainably.

Batch Cooking and Storage Tips

Embracing a whole food plant-based diet is an exciting journey that often requires a bit of strategy, especially when it comes to meal preparation. Batch cooking is a fantastic technique that not only saves time but also ensures that you have healthy, homemade meals ready at a moment's notice. This method allows you to prepare large quantities of food at once, which can then be stored and used throughout the week. Coupled with effective storage techniques, batch cooking can transform your eating habits, making it easier to stick to a healthy diet even on your busiest days.

The Basics of Batch Cooking

Batch cooking starts with planning. Begin by choosing a day when you have a few hours to cook—many find that the weekend works best. Plan your meals around whole grains, legumes, and vegetables, which are all staples of the plant-based diet and also happen to store well. For example, you might cook a big pot of quinoa, a large batch of black bean soup, and roast a tray of mixed vegetables. You can combine these ingredients in various ways to craft diverse meals throughout the week, ensuring both variety and nutritional balance. When preparing your meals, consider the versatility of each component. For example, quinoa might serve as a side dish one evening, feature in a salad the next day, and transform into a breakfast porridge later in the week. This approach not only maximizes the use of your ingredients but also keeps your diet interesting and well-rounded.

Similarly, roasted vegetables can be a dinner side, a salad topping, or a great addition to a wrap. This approach not only maximizes the use of your ingredients but also keeps mealtime interesting.

Effective Storage Solutions

Proper storage is key to maintaining the freshness and nutritional quality of your cooked foods. Invest in good quality airtight containers that can go from fridge to freezer to microwave. Glass containers are especially useful because they don't harbor smells or stains and are generally safer for reheating food than plastic.

Before storing, it's crucial to cool your food promptly. Directly placing hot food in the refrigerator may increase the internal temperature, potentially jeopardizing other stored items. To facilitate faster cooling, divide large amounts of food into smaller, shallow containers. This helps prevent heat from being trapped and speeds up the cooling process, ensuring food safety.

Once cool, seal them tightly and label them with the date. This will help you keep track of what you have and ensure that you use older items first.

Freezing is also an excellent option for extending the life of your batch-cooked meals. Most cooked grains, soups, and stews freeze well. When freezing, leave a small space at the top of the container as foods often expand when frozen. To thaw, transfer the container to the refrigerator the night before you plan to eat it, or reheat it directly from frozen.

Maximizing Flavor and Freshness

To keep meals tasty, consider adding dressings or sauces right before serving rather than before storing. This keeps meals vibrant and prevents dishes from becoming soggy. For instance, if you've made a big batch of a grain salad, add the dressing to the portion you plan to eat immediately and store the rest undressed.

Herbs and spices are your allies in keeping batch-cooked meals exciting. Many herbs, like cilantro or basil, are best added fresh, just before serving, to preserve their flavor and color. Spices can be rejuvenated with a quick toss in a hot pan before sprinkling them onto your reheated dish, which can help release their aromatic oils and revive flavors.

Embracing Flexibility and Creativity

Finally, while batch cooking is about planning and preparation, it also allows for flexibility. Having a variety of cooked base ingredients at your disposal means you can be creative with what you have on hand. If you find yourself with extra vegetables towards the end of the week, consider blending them into a soup or curry. If you have grains and some greens, toss them together for a quick stir-fry.

Batch cooking and effective storage are about making your plant-based diet manageable, enjoyable, and varied. By investing a few hours each week into preparing your meals, you ensure that you have nutritious, plant-rich meals readily available, making it easier to maintain healthy eating habits without stress or last-minute decisions. As you continue to explore and adapt to your plant-based diet, these practices not only simplify your meal prep but also enrich your daily eating experience, keeping it as nourishing as it is delightful.

Creating Balanced Meals

Crafting balanced meals is an art form that centers not only on combining flavors but also on ensuring that each dish provides the nutrients necessary to fuel the body effectively. For those following a whole food plant-based diet, this can seem daunting at first; however, it's an opportunity to get creative with a cornucopia of grains, legumes, fruits, vegetables, nuts, and seeds. These elements can be combined in endless ways to satisfy both nutritional needs and taste buds.

Foundations of a Plant-Based Plate

When thinking about constructing a meal, it helps to visualize the plate divided into components. A well-balanced plant-based meal typically includes a good portion of vegetables, a serving of whole grains, a protein source from legumes or seeds, and a small amount of healthy fats. Vegetables—both raw and cooked—should cover about half the plate. This not only ensures a high intake of fiber and vitamins but also adds volume and color to the meal, enhancing its visual appeal and satisfaction level.

Whole grains like brown rice, quinoa, or whole wheat pasta form the next quarter of the plate. These are excellent sources of complex carbohydrates, giving you sustained energy and providing essential B-vitamins and minerals. The final quarter should include protein sources such as beans, lentils, chickpeas, or tofu. These protein-rich foods are vital for muscle repair, hormone production, and overall cellular health. Incorporating a variety of protein sources throughout the week can help maintain an amino acid balance and keep meals interesting.

Balancing Flavors and Textures

A satisfying meal appeals to a variety of senses, including taste and texture. Balancing flavors—sweet, salty, sour, bitter, and umami—can turn simple dishes into culinary delights. Sweetness from ripe tomatoes or bell peppers can counterbalance the slight bitterness of kale or arugula. A squeeze of lemon or lime adds a sour edge that can lift the entire dish, while a sprinkle of sea salt enhances natural flavors and adds a crunchy texture. Umami, which gives a savory depth to dishes, can be achieved through ingredients like mushrooms, ripe tomatoes, nutritional yeast, and fermented foods like sauerkraut or tamari.

Textural contrasts can also make meals more satisfying. Think of the crunch of raw seeds sprinkled over a smooth soup or creamy avocado slices on top of a crisp salad. These contrasts not only make the meal more enjoyable to eat but can also help you feel more satiated.

Using Herbs and Spices

Herbs and spices are the secret weapons in your pantry, capable of transforming a bland dish into a burst of flavor without the need for extra salt or fat. They also pack a range of antioxidants and health benefits. For instance, turmeric contains curcumin, known for its anti-inflammatory properties, while cinnamon can help regulate blood sugar levels. Fresh herbs like basil, cilantro, and parsley add a fresh burst of flavor and color just before serving, keeping their nutrients intact.

Mindful Meal Prep

Mindfulness in meal preparation means considering not just the nutritional content but also the sustainability of the foods you choose. Opt for seasonal and locally grown produce when possible, which tends to be fresher and more flavorful, and supports local economies. Being mindful also means being aware of food waste—using vegetable scraps for stock or turning overripe fruits into smoothies or compotes.

Intuitive Eating and Flexibility

Finally, balanced eating isn't just about the composition of your meals but also about listening to your body and its needs. Some days, you might crave more hearty, starchy vegetables, while other times, fresh fruits and salads might appeal more. Allowing yourself the flexibility to adapt your meals based on your body's signals is a key part of maintaining a healthy, balanced diet over the long term.

Creating balanced meals is a dynamic and enjoyable part of a whole food plant-based lifestyle. It's about more than just following nutritional guidelines—it's about exploring new foods, experimenting with flavors, and learning to listen to your body's needs. Each meal is an opportunity to nourish yourself creatively and conscientiously, making mealtime both a delight and a powerful tool for maintaining optimal health.

Chapter 5: Addressing Common Challenges

Overcoming Cravings and Maintaining Motivation

Transitioning to a whole food plant-based diet isn't just a change in what you eat; it's a transformation in how you think about food. One of the most common hurdles in this journey involves managing cravings for familiar comfort foods and maintaining the motivation to stick with new eating habits. Understanding why we crave certain foods and developing strategies to stay motivated can help smooth this transition and make the changes more sustainable.

Understanding Cravings

Cravings are a normal part of human physiology, often linked to our emotions, environment, and even nutrient deficiencies. Foods high in fat, sugar, or salt can trigger the brain's reward centers, releasing chemicals like dopamine that make us feel good temporarily. When you switch to a plant-based diet, you might miss these 'highs' from less healthy foods, especially during the initial phase.

To overcome these cravings, start by enriching your diet with plant-based foods that are not only nutritious but also satisfying. Incorporate wholesome fats from avocados, nuts, and seeds, which can help stabilize blood sugar levels and suppress cravings. Sweet vegetables like carrots, beets, and sweet potatoes can naturally satisfy your desire for sweetness. Spices like cinnamon, nutmeg, and vanilla can also add a sweet note to dishes without the need for added sugar.

Creating Satisfying Meals

Another way to manage cravings is to ensure your meals are fulfilling both in terms of nutrition and sensory satisfaction. A bland salad might leave you wanting more, but a hearty, spice-rich lentil soup or a vibrant stir-fry packed with vegetables and tofu can be deeply satisfying. Focus on variety, colors, and fresh flavors to keep your meals interesting and crave-worthy.

Maintaining Motivation

Staying motivated is crucial, especially when the initial excitement of starting a new diet wanes. Set clear, manageable goals and remind yourself why you chose to adopt a plant-based diet. Whether it's for health reasons, ethical considerations, or environmental concerns, reconnecting with your motivations can help reinforce your commitment when challenges arise.

Building a Support Network

Surrounding yourself with supportive friends, family, or online communities who share your dietary goals can also play a significant role in maintaining motivation. Sharing experiences, challenges, and successes with others can provide encouragement and new ideas for recipes or coping strategies.

Learning and Experimenting

Take time to learn about the nutritional aspects of your new diet and experiment with new ingredients and cooking techniques. The more skilled and knowledgeable you become, the more empowered and motivated you'll feel. Cooking classes, nutrition workshops, and plant-based cookbooks can be excellent resources.

Managing Social Situations

Social situations can pose challenges, from dinners out to family gatherings. Plan ahead by checking restaurant menus online, suggesting dining spots with plant-based options, or offering to bring a dish to share when visiting friends or family. Communicating your dietary preferences clearly and confidently can also help manage expectations and minimize discomfort.

Embracing Flexibility

Lastly, be flexible with yourself. If you give in to a craving, don't see it as a failure; instead, use it as a learning experience to better understand your triggers and how to manage them next time. Flexibility can prevent feelings of deprivation, which might otherwise undermine your motivation.

In overcoming cravings and maintaining motivation, remember that every meal is a new opportunity to nourish your body and align with your values. Each choice you make strengthens your commitment and builds resilience, paving the way for lasting change. As you continue on this journey, you will likely find that cravings diminish and motivation becomes more intrinsic as the benefits of a plant-based lifestyle become more apparent and rewarding.

Eating Out and Social Situations

Navigating social situations while maintaining a whole food plant-based diet can seem daunting at first. Whether you're dining at a restaurant, attending a family gathering, or enjoying a night out with friends, the challenge is not just about finding something to eat—it's also about participating fully without feeling excluded. However, with some preparation and thoughtful strategies, these occasions can still be enjoyable and stress-free.

Preparation is Key

When planning to eat out, a little research goes a long way. Most restaurants now offer their menus online, allowing you to scout out potential options beforehand. Look for dishes that are naturally plant-based or can be easily modified. Don't hesitate to call the restaurant ahead of time to ask about plant-based options. Chefs are often willing to accommodate dietary preferences, especially if they receive a heads-up before you arrive.

For social gatherings, communicating your dietary preferences clearly to your host can prevent any awkwardness and ensure there's something on the menu for you. Offering to bring a dish not only eases the burden on your host but also guarantees that you'll have something hearty to enjoy, and it introduces others to plant-based eating.

Navigating Menu Options
Once at the restaurant, focus on the sides or appetizer sections of the menu, as these are often where you'll find plant-based gems hidden among the standard fare. Salads can be a good option, but ensure they're filling enough, or consider pairing with a side of steamed vegetables or a portion of hearty grains like quinoa or farro. If the main dishes are limited, look at combining several side dishes to create a balanced meal.

Socializing Without Stress
Social situations are about connection, not just food. Shift the focus from what you're eating to the joy of spending time with others. If food choices become a topic, use it as an opportunity to share why you've chosen a plant-based lifestyle, focusing on the positives rather than limitations. Most people will be curious rather than critical, and conversations can open more doors than they close.

Handling Questions and Comments
It's common to face questions or even skepticism about your diet choices. Prepare some polite, concise responses about why you eat the way you do, focusing on personal health benefits or ethical reasons if you're comfortable. You can say something like, "I've found eating plant-based really boosts my energy and I enjoy it!" This usually satisfies casual inquiries without leading to a debate.

Cultural Considerations
In many cultures, food is a significant part of social interaction and familial bonds. If your dietary choices are different from traditional family dishes, approach this with sensitivity and respect. Explain your choices in the context of personal health benefits or environmental concerns, which can often resonate more universally than one might expect.

Enjoying Alcohol
If alcohol is part of your social life, it's worth noting that not all alcoholic beverages are vegan due to processing methods. Wines and beers, for instance, can be clarified with animal products. Many companies, however, are starting to label their products or provide information online. Opt for clearly labeled vegan options or stick to simple distilled spirits mixed with plant-based mixers.

Being Flexible
While it's important to stick to your principles, flexibility can sometimes make social interactions smoother. If options are severely limited, focusing on the non-food aspects of the event can help maintain social bonds while you navigate your dietary choices.

Reflecting on Experiences
After dining out or attending an event, take some time to reflect on what went well and what could be improved next time. Perhaps a certain restaurant was particularly accommodating, or maybe a conversation with a friend opened up new perspectives on plant-based eating. Use these insights to refine your approach in future situations. Navigating eating out and socializing on a plant-based diet enriches your social experiences and often leads to deeper understanding and respect for your lifestyle choices. With each positive encounter, you become more adept at managing social situations, ensuring that your dietary choices enhance rather than complicate your social life.

Adopting a whole food plant-based diet is a profoundly healthful decision, but like any diet, it requires thoughtful planning to ensure it provides all the necessary nutrients. Some people worry about potential nutritional deficiencies when eliminating animal products. Adopting a plant-based diet is entirely feasible with appropriate knowledge and planning, ensuring that you don't lack any critical nutrients.

Common Nutritional Concerns

Protein: One of the predominant concerns with plant-based diets is obtaining adequate protein. Contrary to popular belief, protein deficiency is uncommon if your diet is calorically sufficient and varied. Excellent sources of plant-based protein include lentils, beans, tofu, tempeh, and quinoa. Incorporating a diverse array of these foods is crucial as it ensures that you get all essential amino acids needed throughout the day.

Vitamin B12: This is a critical nutrient that is often missing from plant-based diets because it does not naturally occur in plant foods. B12 is essential for nerve function, DNA production, and the formation of red blood cells. To maintain adequate B12 levels, you should regularly consume fortified foods or consider taking a supplement, especially if your diet excludes all animal products.

Regularly including fortified plant milks, cereals, and nutritional yeast, or taking a B12 supplement, can easily meet your needs. Iron and omega-3 fatty acids are pivotal nutrients, particularly in a plant-based diet, and ensuring adequate intake is crucial for maintaining health.

Enhancing Iron Absorption

Iron is vital for numerous bodily functions, including oxygen transport and energy production. While plant-based diets often include many sources of iron, such as lentils, chickpeas, beans, tofu, cashews, and seeds like chia, linseed, and hemp, the type of iron in these foods (non-heme iron) is not absorbed as efficiently as the heme iron found in animal products. To improve iron absorption, it's beneficial to consume vitamin C-rich foods alongside iron-rich foods. Examples of vitamin C-rich foods include bell peppers, citrus fruits, and strawberries, which can significantly enhance the body's ability to absorb iron from plant sources.

Omega-3 Fatty Acids from Plant Sources

Omega-3 fatty acids are essential for brain health and reducing inflammation, and they can be adequately sourced from a plant-based diet. Alpha-linolenic acid (ALA) is a type of omega-3 fat found abundantly in flaxseeds, chia seeds, hemp seeds, and walnuts. While ALA is not as directly beneficial as the EPA and DHA found in fish oils, the body can convert ALA to these more active forms, although the conversion rate is low. Including a variety of these seeds and nuts can help meet the recommended intakes of omega-3 fats to support overall health. For those who want a direct source of EPA and DHA, which are the forms of omega-3 typically found in fish, algae-based supplements are an effective option. Calcium is crucial not only for maintaining strong bones but also for its roles in cardiovascular and muscular functions. A diverse range of plant-based foods can supply calcium, ensuring that those on a plant-based diet can meet their daily requirements without the need for dairy products.

Plant-Based Sources of Calcium

Fortified Plant Milks: Many plant milks such as almond, soy, and oat are fortified with calcium, making them excellent dairy-free alternatives to cow's milk. Tofu: Tofu made with calcium sulfate is an excellent source of calcium. Incorporating tofu into meals can significantly boost calcium intake. Leafy Greens: Dark, leafy greens like collard greens, kale, and bok choy have high calcium content. These vegetables are not only versatile in recipes but also provide additional nutrients like fiber and vitamins A, C, and K. Almonds: Almonds are among the nuts highest in calcium and also provide healthy fats, protein, and vitamin E.

Maximizing Calcium Absorption

To enhance calcium absorption, it is advisable to consume these foods throughout the day. The body has a limited capacity to absorb calcium at one time, so spreading out calcium-rich foods across meals can optimize absorption and utilization. Additionally, factors like vitamin D status and overall diet quality can influence calcium absorption, emphasizing the importance of a well-rounded dietary approach.

Practical Strategies for Nutrient Intake Adopting a tracking habit for a short period can be useful when you're starting a plant-based diet. Tools and apps that track nutritional intake can help you learn about the composition of different foods and understand where there might be gaps in your diet. Regular blood tests are another practical approach. They can help monitor levels of critical nutrients like B12, vitamin D, and iron. If a deficiency is spotted, you'll be able to respond quickly with dietary adjustments or supplements.

Cultural and Culinary Diversity Expanding your culinary repertoire can also prevent nutritional gaps. Different cultures emphasize different plant-based ingredients, providing a broader spectrum of nutrients. Exploring international cuisines can introduce you to new and nutritious foods that you might not otherwise encounter.

Educating Yourself and Others Understanding the nutrients in your food and how they affect your body is crucial. This knowledge not only helps you manage your own diet but also equips you to have informed discussions with friends, family, or healthcare providers who may have questions or concerns about your dietary choices.

Community and Support Engaging with a community of like-minded eaters can provide support and insight. Community resources can offer new recipe ideas that can help you add nutritional diversity to your meals and share ways others have successfully managed potential deficiencies.

Continued Learning and Adaptation A plant-based diet is dynamic; nutritional science is continually evolving, and personal health needs can change over time. Staying informed about the latest research and being open to adjusting your diet in response to new information or changes in your health will help you maintain a balanced and healthful diet. Managing nutritional needs on a plant-based diet is entirely feasible and can be quite enjoyable. With a proactive approach to nutrition, the plant-based journey can be both a delicious and deeply nourishing lifestyle.

Chapter 6: Enhancing Your Whole Food Plant-Based Journey

Incorporating Superfoods into Your Diet

Embracing a whole food plant-based diet opens up a universe of diverse, nutrient-dense foods often labeled as "superfoods." These foods are renowned for their rich nutrient profiles and beneficial health effects. While no individual food can single-handedly guarantee good health or disease prevention, incorporating a diverse array of these superfoods into your diet can enhance your overall nutritional intake and contribute to a healthy eating pattern. Adding such variety also makes meals more enjoyable and interesting, encouraging a sustainable approach to healthy eating.

What Makes a Superfood?

The term "superfood" is not a scientific one but a marketing term that has caught the attention of health-conscious consumers. Generally, it refers to foods that are exceptionally rich in vitamins, minerals, antioxidants, and other health-promoting compounds. Examples within a plant-based context include berries, dark leafy greens, nuts, seeds, and ancient grains, among others.

Berries: Little Powerhouses

Berries, including blueberries, strawberries, raspberries, and blackberries, are nutritional jewels packed with vitamins, fiber, and notably high levels of antioxidants. These small fruits are associated with a wide array of health benefits, such as reducing inflammation and providing protection against heart disease and certain types of cancer. To integrate berries into your diet, try incorporating them into smoothies, oatmeal, or salads, or simply enjoy them as a delicious, low-calorie snack.

Dark Leafy Greens: The Nutrient All-Stars

Dark leafy greens, such as kale, spinach, swiss chard, and collard greens, are powerhouses of nutrition, rich in vitamins A, C, K, and numerous B vitamins. Their dense nutrient content supports a myriad of health benefits, making them an essential part of a balanced diet. They can be easily added to a variety of dishes, including smoothies, soups, and stews, or enjoyed in salads and as steamed or sautéed side dishes, providing a robust boost of nutrients with minimal calories. They also offer minerals like iron, calcium, potassium, and magnesium. Their high antioxidant content makes them powerful allies in fighting inflammation and protecting vascular health. To maximize their benefits and variety in your diet, try adding greens to smoothies, soups, and stews, or enjoy them in salads and as steamed side dishes.

Nuts and Seeds: Essential Fats and More

Nuts and seeds are more than just great sources of protein and healthy fats; they are also packed with fiber, antioxidants, and various vitamins. Flaxseeds, chia seeds, and hemp seeds are highly regarded for their rich content of omega-3 fatty acids, essential for optimal brain health and effective inflammation management. Additionally, nuts such as almonds, walnuts, and Brazil nuts are valuable for their selenium, zinc, and magnesium content, enhancing overall diet quality with essential minerals that support a variety of bodily functions. Incorporating these seeds and nuts into your diet not only boosts your intake of healthy fats but also provides important minerals necessary for maintaining overall health. Sprinkle seeds on your breakfast cereal, blend them into smoothies, or add nuts to your baking for a nutritious boost.

Ancient Grains: Packed with History and Nutrition

Ancient grains such as quinoa, amaranth, and farro are valued for their nutrient density and have been staples in various cultures for millennia. Whole grains like quinoa, amaranth, and buckwheat are revered in plant-based nutrition for their status as complete proteins—each grain contains all nine essential amino acids. These grains are stellar sources of complex carbohydrates, fiber, iron, magnesium, and B vitamins, which contribute to a balanced and nutritious diet. Their versatility allows them to serve as excellent bases for pilafs, enrich soups, or form the foundation of robust and nourishing salads. Incorporating these grains into meals enhances not only the nutritional content but also the satiety and flavor of various dishes.

Legumes: The Protein Powerhouses

Legumes, including beans, lentils, and chickpeas, are fundamental in plant-based diets not just for their protein but for their broad nutritional contributions, including essential minerals and fiber. Legumes, encompassing beans, lentils, chickpeas, and peas, offer a wealth of health benefits that make them a staple in any nutritious diet. They are particularly noted for their ability to lower cholesterol levels, stabilize blood sugar, and potentially reduce the risk of certain cancers. To keep meals varied and nutritionally rich, it's beneficial to include a diverse range of legumes in your diet.

Incorporating Superfoods into Daily Eating

Adding superfoods to your daily meals is simpler than it might seem. These nutrient-dense foods can easily be integrated into your diet without requiring extensive preparation or changes to your existing meal plans. It starts with making small changes—switching out a snack for a handful of nuts, choosing whole grains instead of refined ones, or opting for a berry dessert instead of something sugar-laden. Over time, these choices become a natural part of your eating habits.

Listening to Your Body

As you introduce more superfoods into your diet, pay attention to how your body responds. The increased intake of fiber and nutrients might require some adjustments. Stay hydrated and give your body time to adapt to the changes in your diet.

A Balanced Approach to Superfoods

While superfoods can enhance your diet, they are most effective when consumed as part of a broader, balanced diet rather than in isolation or as a quick fix. No single food can provide all the necessary nutrients for health. Instead, the focus should be on a diverse and colorful diet that includes a wide range of vegetables, fruits, grains, nuts, and seeds. Incorporating superfoods into your plant-based journey is a delightful way to explore new flavors and foods while boosting your nutrient intake. Each meal offers an opportunity to nourish your body deeply and deliciously.

The Role of Exercise and Hydration

Embarking on a whole food plant-based diet is a pivotal step towards better health, but it's only one piece of the wellness puzzle. To truly thrive, this dietary approach should be complemented by regular exercise and proper hydration, both of which play critical roles in maintaining optimal health. When combined, these elements can enhance the benefits of a plant-based diet, leading to improved energy levels, better physical and mental health, and an overall enhanced quality of life.

Integrating Exercise into Your Routine

Exercise is a powerful tool that supports cardiovascular health, strengthens muscles, enhances flexibility, and improves mood and mental health. For those adopting a plant-based lifestyle, incorporating a regular exercise regimen can also help manage weight, increase metabolism, and optimize nutrient utilization from the diet.

The exercise you select should align with your personal preferences, fitness level, and overall health objectives. Aerobic activities, such as walking, running, cycling, or swimming, are particularly beneficial for cardiovascular health and improving endurance. Additionally, strength training—whether through weights, resistance bands, or body-weight exercises—is crucial for maintaining bone density, muscle mass, and metabolic rate. Flexibility and balance exercises, such as yoga or Pilates, are equally important as they not only support joint health but also contribute to mental well-being.

It's crucial to choose exercises that you find enjoyable and can commit to on a regular basis. When starting out, consistency is more critical than intensity. Experts recommend engaging in at least 150 minutes of moderate aerobic activity or 75 minutes of vigorous activity per week, supplemented by strength training on two or more days each week.

The Importance of Hydration

Hydration is essential for the optimal functioning of every system in your body, including the heart, brain, and muscles. Adequate hydration aids in detoxification, delivers nutrients to cells, helps regulate body temperature, and maintains moist and healthy tissues.

When you're following a plant-based diet, hydration becomes even more crucial due to the increased fiber intake. Fiber plays a critical role in digestion by absorbing water, so it's essential to increase your water intake to facilitate this process and prevent digestive discomforts such as bloating and constipation. The specific amount of water you need can vary depending on factors like your level of physical activity, the climate you live in, and your overall health.

A practical method to ensure you're adequately hydrated is to observe the color of your urine; it should be a light yellow. To maintain steady hydration levels, it's best to drink water consistently throughout the day instead of consuming large amounts all at once. Additionally, incorporating foods that are rich in water content, such as cucumbers, tomatoes, oranges, and melons, can further enhance your hydration status.

Exercise, Hydration, and Plant-Based Nutrition

Combining exercise with a plant-based diet enhances nutrient absorption. For instance, cardiovascular exercise improves blood flow, helping to more efficiently transport the vitamins and minerals you consume into the bloodstream. Similarly, regular movement increases muscle mass, which can improve insulin sensitivity, an important factor for managing blood sugar levels.

Proper hydration supports this process by aiding in the transportation of nutrients and oxygen to cells, and by facilitating the removal of waste products from the body. When your body is well-hydrated, you may also notice improved skin health and more consistent energy levels, which can further motivate you to maintain your exercise routine.

Creating a Balanced Lifestyle

Integrating exercise and hydration with your diet isn't just about adding elements to your routine; it's about creating a balanced lifestyle that supports all aspects of your health. Start small, perhaps by taking short walks and gradually increasing the distance and pace, or by trying different types of workouts to see what you enjoy most. Similarly, improve your hydration by carrying a water bottle and setting reminders to drink if you often forget.

Developing these habits alongside your plant-based diet can lead to significant improvements in how you feel both physically and mentally. Exercise and hydration enhance the benefits of a nutritious diet, making it easier to enjoy an active and vibrant life. As you continue to nurture these habits, they become a natural part of your daily routine, reinforcing the positive changes you've made by adopting a plant-based lifestyle.

Mindfulness and Sustainable Eating

Embracing a whole food plant-based diet is a profound step towards health and wellness, but integrating mindfulness and sustainability into your eating habits can elevate this lifestyle change to an even higher level of impact, both personally and environmentally. Mindfulness in eating goes beyond simply choosing plant-based foods; it involves paying attention to how we eat, where our food comes from, and the implications of our food choices on the environment and our communities.

Understanding Mindful Eating

Mindful eating is about experiencing food more intensely—honoring where it comes from, savoring each bite, and appreciating the efforts behind its production. This practice can transform eating from a mere act of consumption into a moment of deep appreciation, creating a more satisfying relationship with food. It encourages us to slow down and eat with intention and attention, noticing the flavors, textures, and aromas of our meals, which can help in regulating appetite and enhancing digestion.

To start practicing mindful eating, begin by reducing distractions at meal times. Turn off the TV, put away your phone, and try to eat in a calm environment where you can focus on your meal. Pay attention to how the food makes you feel and the signals your body sends about hunger and fullness. This awareness can help prevent overeating and ensure that you are truly nourishing your body.

Sustainable Eating Practices

Sustainability in eating involves making food choices that are environmentally friendly, ethically sourced, and economically viable. Embracing a whole food plant-based diet is a powerful step towards sustainability, as such diets generally use fewer resources—like water, land, and energy—compared to diets rich in animal products. To further enhance the eco-friendliness of your dietary choices, consider incorporating practices that lower the environmental impact even more.

Opting for organic and locally sourced produce can significantly reduce the carbon footprint linked to long-distance food transportation. Supporting local agriculture not only cuts down on greenhouse gas emissions but also supports biodiversity and boosts local economies. Engage with your local food system by joining community supported agriculture (CSA) programs or shopping at farmers' markets, which helps forge a closer connection with the source of your food.

Another vital component of sustainable eating involves minimizing food waste. Carefully plan your meals to ensure you utilize all the ingredients you purchase. Properly store leftovers to extend their usability, and compost organic scraps to enrich the soil, closing the nutrient loop in your own backyard. Additionally, being conscious of packaging choices and favoring products with minimal or recyclable packaging can further reduce your ecological footprint, helping to create a healthier planet.

The Role of Community

Engaging with community efforts to promote sustainability can amplify your impact. Participating in local clean-up drives, joining community gardens, or volunteering at food banks are ways to contribute positively while strengthening your commitment to mindful and sustainable eating practices.

Education is also a powerful tool in sustainability. Learn about the practices behind your food, the seasonality of produce, and the benefits of diverse crops. Sharing this knowledge can help others make informed choices about their food, spreading the impact of sustainability further.

Integrating Mindfulness and Sustainability

Integrating mindfulness and sustainability into your eating practices can transform the act of eating into a supportive process for both personal health and environmental health. It fosters a deep sense of connection to your food, the earth, and your community, reinforcing the positive choices you make every day towards a healthier planet.

Each meal then becomes an opportunity not just to nourish your body, but to contribute to a larger cause of environmental stewardship and ethical consumption. By adopting mindful and sustainable eating habits, you're participating in a global movement towards health and sustainability, making choices that benefit not only yourself but also the world around you.

In summary, while each meal is a chance to nourish and delight, approached mindfully and sustainably, it also becomes a gesture of respect and care for the broader web of life that sustains us all. This holistic approach not only enriches your own life but also contributes to a more vibrant, healthful world.

Chapter 7: Breakfast Recipes

TROPICAL GREEN ENERGY SMOOTHIE

PREP: 10 min - COOKING: 0 min
MODE OF COOKING: Blending -
SERVES: 2
GI: Low (~35)

ingr. list:
- 1 ripe avocado, peeled and pitted
- 1 cup fresh spinach leaves
- 1 small banana, sliced and frozen
- 1/2 cup pineapple chunks, frozen
- 1 Tbsp chia seeds
- 1 cup unsweetened almond milk
- 1 tsp fresh ginger, grated
- Ice cubes (optional)

Steps:
Combine avocado, spinach, banana, pineapple, chia seeds, almond milk, and ginger in a blender.
Blend on high until smooth. Add ice cubes for a thicker smoothie if desired.
Serve immediately for optimal freshness and flavor.

Recommendations:
- For a protein boost, add a scoop of your favorite plant-based protein powder.
- Garnish with a sprinkle of chia seeds or a few spinach leaves for an extra touch of green.

Nutritional Values: Calories: 245, Fat: 15g, Carbs: 27g, Protein: 4g, Sugar: 12g

TOASTED QUINOA AND AVOCADO BREAKY BOWL

PREP: 15 min - COOKING: 10 min
MODE OF COOKING: Sautéing -
SERVES: 2
GI: Low (~40)

Ingredient List:
- 1/2 cup quinoa (uncooked)
- 1 ripe avocado, diced
- 1/4 cup cherry tomatoes, halved
- 1 small cucumber, diced
- 2 Tbsp hemp seeds
- 1 Tbsp olive oil
- 1 tsp lemon juice
- Salt and pepper to taste
- Fresh parsley or cilantro, chopped (for garnish)

Steps:
1. In a dry skillet over medium heat, toast the quinoa for 2-3 minutes, stirring frequently until golden and fragrant. Remove from heat and set aside.
2. Cook the quinoa according to package instructions. Once cooked, fluff with a fork and allow it to cool slightly.
3. In a bowl, combine the cooked quinoa, diced avocado, cherry tomatoes, and cucumber.
4. Drizzle with olive oil and lemon juice, and season with salt and pepper to taste.
5. Sprinkle hemp seeds on top and garnish with fresh parsley or cilantro.

Recommendations:
- Add a handful of arugula or spinach for extra greens and fiber.
- Serve with a side of fruit or a green smoothie for a complete breakfast.

Nutritional Values:
Calories: 320, Fat: 18g, Carbs: 35g, Protein: 9g, Sugar: 3g

SPICED PUMPKIN SMOOTHIE

PREP: 10 min - COOKING: 0 min
MODE OF COOKING: Blending -
SERVES: 2
GI: Low (~40)
ingr. list:
• 1 cup pumpkin puree, chilled
• 1 large apple, cored and quartered
• 1/2 banana, frozen
• 1/2 tsp ground cinnamon
• 1/4 tsp ground nutmeg
• 1/4 tsp ground ginger
• 1 Tbsp almond butter
• 1 cup unsweetened soy milk
• Ice cubes (optional)
Steps:
Place all ingredients into a blender, adding ice if a colder smoothie is desired.
Blend on high until creamy and smooth. Taste and adjust spices if necessary, then blend again briefly.
Recommendations:
• Serve immediately, topped with a sprinkle of cinnamon or nut flakes for an autumn-inspired touch.
• For a sweeter smoothie, add a teaspoon of maple syrup or agave nectar.
Nutritional Values: Calories: 200, Fat: 8g, Carbs: 28g, Protein: 6g, Sugar: 15g

AVOCADO CITRUS SMOOTHIE

PREP: 10 min - COOKING: 0 min
MODE OF COOKING: Blending -
SERVES: 2
GI: Low (~30)
ingr. list:
• 1 ripe avocado, peeled and pitted
• 1/2 grapefruit, peeled and seeded
• 1 orange, peeled and seeded
• 1/2 lime, juice only
• 1 Tbsp hemp seeds
• 1 cup water or coconut water
• Ice cubes (optional)
Steps:
Combine avocado, grapefruit, orange, lime juice, hemp seeds, and water in a blender.
Add ice if desired for a chilled smoothie.
Blend on high until completely smooth.
Taste and add a touch of agave syrup if a sweeter flavor is desired.
Recommendations:
• Garnish with a slice of lime or orange on the glass for a refreshing citrus twist.
• Great post-workout for its good fats and quick energy from natural sugars.
Nutritional Values: Calories: 210, Fat: 15g, Carbs: 20g, Protein: 4g, Sugar: 8g

GOLDEN TURMERIC SMOOTHIE BOWL

PREP: 15 min - COOKING: 0 min
MODE OF COOKING: Blending -
SERVES: 1
GI: Low (~50)
ingr. list:
• 1 cup frozen mango chunks
• 1/2 banana, sliced and frozen

- 1/2 tsp turmeric powder
- 1/4 tsp ground cinnamon
- Pinch of black pepper (to enhance turmeric absorption)
- 1 Tbsp chia seeds
- 1 cup unsweetened almond milk
- 1 Tbsp coconut flakes

Steps:
Place mango, banana, turmeric, cinnamon, black pepper, chia seeds, and almond milk into a blender.
Blend until smooth; pour into a bowl.
Sprinkle coconut flakes over the top before serving.

Recommendations:
- Add a scoop of plant-based protein powder to turn this into a power breakfast.
- Decorate with additional banana slices or a few edible flowers for an Instagram-worthy presentation.

Nutritional Values: Calories: 320, Fat: 10g, Carbs: 55g, Protein: 5g, Sugar: 35g

MINTY MELON SMOOTHIE

PREP: 10 min - COOKING: 0 min
MODE OF COOKING: Blending -
SERVES: 2
GI: Low (~35)

ingr. list:
- 2 cups cubed honeydew melon
- 1/2 cucumber, peeled and sliced
- 12 fresh mint leaves
- 1 Tbsp lime juice
- 1 cup spinach leaves
- 1/2 cup plain unsweetened almond milk
- Ice cubes (optional)

Steps:
Combine honeydew, cucumber, mint leaves, lime juice, spinach, and almond milk in a blender.
Add ice if desired for a cooler drink.
Blend until smooth and frothy.
Serve immediately, garnished with extra mint leaves or a lime wedge.

Recommendations:
- Perfect for a refreshing summer morning. The cucumber and melon provide hydration while mint energizes.
- For an extra kick, add a pinch of ginger or a scoop of green tea matcha powder.

Nutritional Values: Calories: 120, Fat: 1g, Carbs: 26g, Protein: 3g, Sugar: 20g

ALMOND OAT BANANA PANCAKES

PREP: 10 min - **COOKING:** 15 min
MODE OF COOKING: Pan frying -
SERVES: 4

Ingr. list:
- 1 cup oat flour
- 1/2 cup almond flour
- 1 Tbsp baking powder
- 1/4 tsp salt
- 1 cup unsweetened almond milk
- 2 ripe bananas, mashed
- 1 Tbsp maple syrup
- 1 tsp vanilla extract
- Coconut oil, for cooking

Steps:
In a bowl, mix oat flour, almond flour, baking powder, and salt.
Stir in almond milk, mashed bananas, maple syrup, and vanilla extract until smooth.
Heat a non-stick skillet and brush with coconut oil. Pour 1/4 cup of batter for each pancake.
Cook over medium heat until bubbles form on the surface, then flip and cook until golden.

Recommendations:
- Serve with fresh berries and a drizzle of additional maple syrup.
- Add a pinch of cinnamon to the batter for a warm flavor.

Nutritional Values: Calories: 210, Fat: 9g, Carbs: 30g, Protein: 6g, Sugar: 8g

ZUCCHINI OAT WAFFLES

PREP: 15 min - **COOKING:** 20 min
MODE OF COOKING: Baking in a waffle iron - **SERVES:** 4
Ingr. list:
• 1 1/2 cups rolled oats
• 1/2 cup grated zucchini
• 1 Tbsp ground flaxseed mixed with 3 Tbsp water
• 1 1/4 cups unsweetened soy milk
• 2 Tbsp olive oil
• 1 tsp baking powder
• 1/2 tsp salt
• 1/2 tsp garlic powder
• 1/4 tsp ground black pepper
Steps:
Pulse oats in a blender until they resemble a coarse flour.
Mix flaxseed with water and set aside to thicken for 5 min.
Combine all ingredients, including the flaxseed mixture, in a bowl and stir until well combined.
Preheat a waffle iron and grease lightly with oil. Pour batter and cook according to the iron's instructions until crisp.
Recommendations:
• Serve with a dollop of vegan sour cream and chives.
• Ideal for a savory breakfast option or a quick lunch.
Nutritional Values: Calories: 250, Fat: 10g, Carbs: 32g, Protein: 8g, Sugar: 2g

BLUEBERRY LEMON PANCAKES

PREP: 10 min - **COOKING:** 15 min
MODE OF COOKING: Pan frying - **SERVES:** 4
Ingr. list:
• 1 cup whole wheat flour
• 1 Tbsp baking powder
• 1/4 tsp salt
• 1 cup unsweetened almond milk
• 1 Tbsp lemon zest
• 1/2 cup fresh blueberries
• 1 Tbsp coconut oil, for cooking
Steps:
In a bowl, mix flour, baking powder, and salt.
Stir in almond milk and lemon zest until the batter is smooth.
Fold in blueberries gently.
Heat a skillet over medium heat, grease with coconut oil, and cook 1/4 cup scoops of batter until bubbles form and edges are dry. Flip and cook until golden.
Recommendations:
• Perfect with a light dusting of powdered sugar or a splash of lemon juice.
• Ensure not to overmix the batter to keep the pancakes fluffy.
Nutritional Values: Calories: 180, Fat: 5g, Carbs: 29g, Protein: 4g, Sugar: 5g

SWEET POTATO AND SPINACH WAFFLES

PREP: 20 min - **COOKING:** 20 min
MODE OF COOKING: Baking in a waffle iron - **SERVES:** 4
Ingr. list:
• 1 large sweet potato, cooked and mashed
• 1 cup spelt flour
• 1 cup baby spinach, finely chopped
• 1 1/4 cups unsweetened almond milk
• 2 tsp baking powder
• 1/2 tsp ground cinnamon
• 1/4 tsp nutmeg
• Olive oil for greasing
Steps:
In a large bowl, combine mashed sweet potato, spelt flour, spinach, almond milk, baking powder, cinnamon, and nutmeg. Mix until smooth.
Preheat your waffle iron and grease it

lightly with olive oil.
Pour in the batter, spread evenly, and cook as per the waffle iron's instructions until crisp and golden.

Recommendations:
• Serve with a light drizzle of agave syrup and a sprinkle of toasted pecans for extra crunch.
• Perfect for a fall breakfast, providing a comforting and filling start to your day.

Nutritional Values: Calories: 290, Fat: 6g, Carbs: 53g, Protein: 8g, Sugar: 7g

---

CINNAMON BUCKWHEAT PANCAKES

PREP: 10 min - **COOKING:** 15 min
MODE OF COOKING: Pan frying -
SERVES: 4
Ingr. list:
• 1 cup buckwheat flour
• 1 Tbsp ground cinnamon
• 1 Tbsp baking powder
• 1/4 tsp salt
• 1 1/4 cups unsweetened almond milk
• 2 Tbsp maple syrup
• 1 tsp vanilla extract
• Coconut oil, for cooking

Steps:
In a mixing bowl, combine buckwheat flour, cinnamon, baking powder, and salt.
Add almond milk, maple syrup, and vanilla extract. Stir until smooth.
Heat a non-stick pan over medium heat, lightly grease with coconut oil, and pour 1/4 cup batter per pancake.
Cook until bubbles appear on the surface, then flip and cook until browned on the other side.

Recommendations:
• Top with sliced bananas and a drizzle of extra maple syrup for a sweet breakfast treat.
• Buckwheat flour provides a hearty texture and nutty flavor that pairs well with cinnamon.

Nutritional Values: Calories: 175, Fat: 3g, Carbs: 34g, Protein: 4g, Sugar: 8g

CHOCOLATE CHIP OATMEAL WAFFLES

PREP: 15 min - **COOKING:** 20 min
MODE OF COOKING: Baking in a waffle iron - **SERVES:** 4
Ingr. list:
• 1 1/2 cups oat flour
• 1/2 cup rolled oats
• 1/4 cup raw cacao nibs or mini vegan chocolate chips
• 2 tsp baking powder
• 1/4 tsp salt
• 1 1/2 cups unsweetened almond milk
• 2 Tbsp melted coconut oil
• 1 Tbsp maple syrup
Steps:
Mix oat flour, rolled oats, cacao nibs, baking powder, and salt in a large bowl. Stir in almond milk, coconut oil, and maple syrup until the batter is well combined.
Preheat a waffle iron and grease it with a little coconut oil. Pour the batter into the iron and cook according to the manufacturer's instructions until crisp and golden.
Recommendations:
• Serve with a dollop of almond butter and fresh raspberries for a decadent breakfast.
• The combination of oats and chocolate provides a satisfying and slightly indulgent start to the day.
Nutritional Values: Calories: 260, Fat: 12g, Carbs: 33g, Protein: 5g, Sugar: 7g

SAVORY QUINOA AND KALE BREAKFAST BOWL

PREP: 10 min - **COOKING:** 20 min
MODE OF COOKING: Simmering - **SERVES:** 2
GI: Medium (~50)
Ingr. list:
• 1 cup quinoa, rinsed
• 2 cups vegetable broth
• 2 cups chopped kale
• 1/2 cup cherry tomatoes, halved
• 1/4 cup red onion, finely chopped
• 2 Tbsp olive oil
• 1 tsp garlic powder
• Salt and pepper to taste
• 4 Tbsp nutritional yeast
Steps:
In a medium saucepan, bring quinoa and vegetable broth to a boil. Reduce heat, cover, and simmer for 15 min. Stir in chopped kale, cover, and cook for an additional 5 min until quinoa is fluffy and kale is wilted.
In a small skillet, sauté cherry tomatoes and red onion in olive oil until onions are translucent.
Mix sautéed vegetables into the quinoa-kale mixture. Season with garlic powder, salt, and pepper.
Serve hot, sprinkled with nutritional yeast for a cheesy flavor.
Recommendations:
• Add a drizzle of tahini or a squeeze of lemon juice for extra zest.
• Top with avocado slices for healthy fats and a creamy texture.
Nutritional Values: Calories: 310, Fat: 10g, Carbs: 45g, Protein: 12g, Sugar: 4g

TEMPEH SCRAMBLE TACO BOWL

PREP: 10 min - **COOKING**: 10 min
MODE OF COOKING: Sautéing -
SERVES: 4
GI: Low (~40)

Ingr. list:
- 14 oz tempeh, crumbled
- 1 Tbsp olive oil
- 1/2 tsp turmeric
- 1 tsp cumin
- 1/2 tsp chili powder
- 1 bell pepper, diced
- 1 small red onion, diced
- Salt and pepper to taste
- 4 corn tortillas, warmed
- Fresh cilantro for garnish

Steps:
1. Heat olive oil in a large skillet over medium heat. Add crumbled tempeh and spices; sauté for 5 min.
2. Add bell pepper and onion; cook until vegetables are tender and tempeh is lightly browned, about 5 min more.
3. Season with salt and pepper.
4. Serve the tempeh scramble in warmed corn tortillas, garnished with fresh cilantro.

Recommendations:
- Serve with a side of salsa and sliced avocado for a full meal.
- Sprinkle with a dash of nutritional yeast for a cheesy flavor without the cheese.

Nutritional Values: Calories: 250, Fat: 10g, Carbs: 25g, Protein: 18g, Sugar: 3g
This substitution should offer a nuttier flavor and more texture compared to tofu.

SWEET POTATO AND BLACK BEAN BREAKFAST HASH

PREP: 15 min - **COOKING:** 20 min
MODE OF COOKING: Pan frying -
SERVES: 4
GI: Medium (~55)

Ingr. list:
- 2 medium sweet potatoes, peeled and diced
- 1 Tbsp olive oil
- 1 cup canned black beans, rinsed and drained
- 1 bell pepper, diced
- 1/2 red onion, diced
- 1 tsp smoked paprika
- 1/2 tsp garlic powder
- Salt and pepper to taste
- Fresh parsley for garnish

Steps:
Heat olive oil in a large skillet over medium heat. Add sweet potatoes; cook until beginning to soften, about 10 min.
Add bell pepper and onion; continue cooking until all vegetables are tender, about 10 more min.
Stir in black beans, smoked paprika, and garlic powder; cook until heated through. Season with salt and pepper.

Serve hot, garnished with chopped fresh parsley.

Recommendations:
• Perfect with a dollop of guacamole or a drizzle of hot sauce for extra kick.
• For added protein, top with a poached egg or extra scoop of black beans.

Nutritional Values: Calories: 290, Fat: 7g, Carbs: 50g, Protein: 8g, Sugar: 7g

MUSHROOM AND SPINACH BREAKFAST BOWL

PREP: 10 min - **COOKING:** 15 min
MODE OF COOKING: Sautéing -
SERVES: 2
GI: Low (~35)
Ingr. list:
• 1 Tbsp olive oil
• 2 cups sliced cremini mushrooms
• 2 cups fresh spinach
• 1 garlic clove, minced
• 1/4 tsp salt
• 1/4 tsp black pepper
• 1/2 tsp dried thyme
• 1/4 cup walnuts, chopped
• 2 Tbsp balsamic vinegar

Steps:
Heat olive oil in a large skillet over medium heat. Add mushrooms and garlic; sauté until mushrooms are golden, about 8 min.
Stir in spinach, salt, pepper, and thyme; cook until spinach is wilted, about 2 min.
Drizzle with balsamic vinegar and sprinkle with chopped walnuts just before serving.

Recommendations:
• Serve with a slice of toasted whole grain bread for a hearty meal.
• For a protein boost, add a scoop of cooked quinoa or a poached egg on top.

Nutritional Values: Calories: 250,

Fat: 18g, Carbs: 18g, Protein: 6g, Sugar: 5g

PEAR AND ALMOND OVERNIGHT OATS

PREP: 10 min - **COOKING:** 0 min (Refrigerate overnight)
MODE OF COOKING: No cook -
SERVES: 2
GI: Low (~40)
Ingr. list:
• 1 cup rolled oats
• 1 cup unsweetened almond milk
• 1 pear, diced
• 1/4 tsp cinnamon
• 2 Tbsp almond butter
• 1 Tbsp chia seeds
• 1 Tbsp maple syrup

Steps:
In a medium bowl, mix together oats, almond milk, chia seeds, and cinnamon.
Stir in diced pear and almond butter. Drizzle with maple syrup and mix well. Cover and refrigerate overnight. Serve chilled.

Recommendations:
• Top with a few slices of fresh pear or a sprinkle of crushed almonds for added texture.
• Customize with your favorite seasonal fruits or nuts according to taste.

Nutritional Values: Calories: 330, Fat: 12g, Carbs: 48g, Protein: 10g, Sugar: 15g

tomato soup or a side of seasoned sweet potato wedges.
• For an extra kick, sprinkle with red pepper flakes or a dash of hot sauce.
Nutritional Values: Calories: 270, Fat: 15g, Carbs: 29g, Protein: 9g, Sugar: 4g

AVOCADO TOAST WITH RADISH AND ARUGULA

PREP: 5 min - **COOKING:** 5 min
MODE OF COOKING: Toasting -
SERVES: 2
GI: Low (~45)
Ingr. list:
• 4 slices whole grain bread
• 1 ripe avocado, mashed
• 1/2 tsp lemon juice
• 1/4 tsp salt
• 1/4 tsp black pepper
• 4 radishes, thinly sliced
• 1 cup arugula
• 1 tsp olive oil
• 1 tsp sesame seeds
Steps:
Toast the bread slices to desired crispness.
In a small bowl, mix mashed avocado with lemon juice, salt, and pepper.
Spread the avocado mixture evenly on the toasted bread.
Top each slice with sliced radishes and arugula, drizzle with olive oil, and sprinkle with sesame seeds.
Recommendations:
• This dish pairs well with a fresh

Chapter 8: Lunch Recipes

CRUNCHY KALE AND APPLE SALAD

PREP: 15 min **MODE OF COOKING:** Raw - **SERVES:** 4
Ingr. list:
• 4 cups kale, stems removed and leaves finely chopped
• 1 large apple, cored and thinly sliced
• 1/4 cup walnuts, chopped
• 1/4 cup dried cranberries
• 2 Tbsp olive oil
• 1 Tbsp apple cider vinegar
• 1 tsp Dijon mustard
• Salt and pepper to taste
Steps:
In a large bowl, combine kale, apple slices, walnuts, and dried cranberries.
In a small bowl, whisk together olive oil, apple cider vinegar, Dijon mustard, salt, and pepper.
Pour dressing over the salad and toss to coat evenly. Let sit for 10 minutes to allow kale to soften.
Recommendations:
• Massage the kale with a bit of olive oil before adding other ingredients to make it tender.
• Try adding a sprinkle of goat cheese or feta for a creamy texture and tangy flavor.
Nutritional Values: Calories: 180, Fat: 10g, Carbs: 22g, Protein: 4g, Sugar: 14g

MEDITERRANEAN QUINOA SALAD

PREP: 20 min - **COOKING:** 15 min
MODE OF COOKING: Boiling - **SERVES:** 4
Ingr. list:
• 1 cup quinoa, rinsed
• 1 cup cherry tomatoes, halved
• 1 cucumber, diced
• 1/2 cup Kalamata olives, pitted and halved
• 1/4 cup red onion, finely chopped
• 1/4 cup feta cheese, crumbled
• 1/4 cup parsley, chopped
• 3 Tbsp olive oil
• 2 Tbsp lemon juice
• 1 garlic clove, minced
• Salt and pepper to taste
Steps:
Cook quinoa according to package instructions; let cool.
In a large bowl, combine cooled quinoa, cherry tomatoes, cucumber, olives, red onion, and parsley.
In a small bowl, whisk together olive oil, lemon juice, minced garlic, salt, and pepper.
Drizzle dressing over the salad and toss to combine. Sprinkle feta cheese on top before serving.
Recommendations:
• Serve chilled or at room temperature.
• Enhance flavor with a sprinkle of dried oregano or mint.
Nutritional Values: Calories: 290, Fat: 18g, Carbs: 27g, Protein: 7g, Sugar: 4g

SPICY LENTIL AND SWEET POTATO SALAD

PREP: 15 min - **COOKING:** 25 min
MODE OF COOKING: Boiling/Roasting - **SERVES:** 4
Ingr. list:
• 1 cup dried green lentils
• 2 medium sweet potatoes, peeled and cubed
• 1 Tbsp olive oil
• 1 tsp smoked paprika
• 1/2 tsp cayenne pepper
• 1 avocado, diced
• 1/4 cup cilantro, chopped
• 3 Tbsp lime juice
• Salt and pepper to taste

Steps:
Cook lentils in boiling water until tender, about 20-25 min; drain well.
Toss sweet potatoes with olive oil, smoked paprika, cayenne pepper, salt, and pepper. Roast in preheated oven at 400°F (204°C) until tender, about 20 min.
In a large bowl, mix cooked lentils, roasted sweet potatoes, avocado, and cilantro.
Drizzle with lime juice and toss to combine.

Recommendations:
• Serve warm or at room temperature.
• For an extra kick, add a chopped jalapeño to the roasting sweet potatoes.

Nutritional Values: Calories: 275, Fat: 9g, Carbs: 40g, Protein: 11g, Sugar: 7g

ASIAN PEAR AND ARUGULA SALAD

PREP: 15 min - **COOKING:** 0 min
MODE OF COOKING: Raw - **SERVES:** 4
Ingr. list:
• 2 Asian pears, thinly sliced
• 4 cups arugula
• 1/2 cup sliced almonds, toasted
• 1/4 cup dried cranberries
• 2 Tbsp sesame oil
• 2 Tbsp rice vinegar
• 1 tsp honey
• 1 tsp soy sauce
• Salt and black pepper to taste

Steps:
In a large salad bowl, combine the arugula, sliced Asian pears, toasted almonds, and dried cranberries.
In a small bowl, whisk together sesame oil, rice vinegar, honey, soy sauce, salt, and pepper.
Drizzle the dressing over the salad and toss gently to coat all ingredients evenly.

Recommendations:
• Chill the pears before slicing for a refreshing crunch.
• Garnish with sesame seeds for an extra nutty flavor and appealing look.

Nutritional Values: Calories: 210, Fat: 14g, Carbs: 20g, Protein: 3g, Sugar: 12g

ROASTED BEET AND GOAT CHEESE SALAD

PREP: 10 min - **COOKING:** 45 min
MODE OF COOKING: Roasting - **SERVES:** 4
Ingr. list:
• 4 medium beets, peeled and cubed
• 1 Tbsp olive oil
• Salt and pepper to taste
• 4 cups mixed greens (spinach, kale, arugula)
• 1/2 cup goat cheese, crumbled
• 1/4 cup pecans, toasted
• 2 Tbsp balsamic vinegar
• 1 Tbsp honey

Steps:
Toss the beets with olive oil, salt, and pepper. Roast in a preheated oven at 375°F (190°C) until tender, about 45 min.
Let beets cool slightly, then mix with the mixed greens, goat cheese, and toasted pecans in a large salad bowl.
In a small bowl, whisk together balsamic vinegar and honey. Drizzle over the salad and toss to combine.

Recommendations:
• Serve immediately while the beets are still warm for a wonderful contrast with the cool greens.
• For a vegan version, substitute goat cheese with vegan cheese or omit it altogether.

Nutritional Values: Calories: 275, Fat: 18g, Carbs: 22g, Protein: 7g, Sugar: 16g

AVOCADO AND BLACK BEAN SALAD

PREP: 20 min - **COOKING:** 0 min
MODE OF COOKING: Raw - **SERVES:** 4

Ingr. list:
• 2 ripe avocados, diced
• 1 can (15 oz) black beans, rinsed and drained
• 1 red bell pepper, diced
• 1/4 cup red onion, finely chopped
• 1/2 cup corn kernels (fresh or frozen and thawed)
• 1/4 cup cilantro, chopped
• 2 Tbsp lime juice
• 1 Tbsp olive oil
• 1 tsp ground cumin
• Salt and pepper to taste

Steps:
In a large bowl, combine avocados, black beans, bell pepper, red onion, and corn.
Add chopped cilantro, lime juice, olive oil, ground cumin, salt, and pepper.
Toss all the ingredients gently until well combined and evenly coated with the dressing.

Recommendations:
• Chill the salad for at least an hour before serving to enhance the flavors.
• Great as a filling for wraps or as a hearty topping for grilled chicken or fish.

Nutritional Values: Calories: 290, Fat: 15g, Carbs: 34g, Protein: 8g, Sugar: 4g

SPICY TOMATO AND LENTIL SOUP

PREP: 10 min - **COOKING:** 40 min
MODE OF COOKING: Simmering -
SERVES: 4

Ingr. list:
• 1 Tbsp olive oil
• 1 onion, chopped
• 2 garlic cloves, minced
• 1 tsp ground cumin
• 1/2 tsp cayenne pepper
• 1 quart vegetable broth
• 1 cup dried red lentils, rinsed
• 2 cups diced tomatoes
• Salt and pepper to taste
• Fresh cilantro, chopped for garnish

Steps:
Heat the olive oil in a large pot over medium heat. Add the onion and garlic, cooking until soft.
Stir in the cumin and cayenne and cook for 1 min. Add the vegetable broth, lentils, and tomatoes.
Bring to a boil, then reduce heat and simmer for 30 min, or until lentils are tender.
Season with salt and pepper. Serve hot, garnished with cilantro.

Recommendations:
• Serve with a dollop of yogurt or a slice of crusty whole-grain bread for a hearty meal.
• For a smoother texture, blend half the soup before serving.

Nutritional Values: Calories: 230, Fat: 5g, Carbs: 35g, Protein: 12g, Sugar: 6g

CREAMY BROCCOLI AND ALMOND SOUP

PREP: 15 min - **COOKING:** 30 min
MODE OF COOKING: Boiling -
SERVES: 4
Ingr. list:
• 1 Tbsp olive oil
• 1 onion, chopped
• 2 cups broccoli florets
• 1/4 cup ground almonds
• 4 cups vegetable broth
• Salt and pepper to taste
• Almond flakes, toasted, for garnish
Steps:
In a pot, heat olive oil over medium heat. Add onion, cooking until translucent.
Add broccoli and ground almonds, cook for 2 min. Pour in vegetable broth and bring to a boil.
Reduce heat, cover, and simmer for 20 min. Puree the soup in batches until smooth.
Return to the pot, season with salt and pepper, and heat through. Serve garnished with toasted almond flakes.
Recommendations:
• For extra creaminess, add a splash of almond milk before serving.
• Garnish with fresh herbs like parsley or thyme for added flavor.
Nutritional Values: Calories: 180, Fat: 11g, Carbs: 16g, Protein: 6g, Sugar: 5g

MOROCCAN SWEET POTATO AND CHICKPEA STEW

PREP: 20 min - **COOKING:** 50 min
MODE OF COOKING: Simmering -
SERVES: 6

Ingr. list:
• 2 Tbsp olive oil
• 1 onion, chopped
• 3 garlic cloves, minced
• 2 tsp ground cumin
• 1 tsp ground cinnamon
• 1/2 tsp cayenne pepper
• 3 large sweet potatoes, peeled and cubed
• 1 quart vegetable broth
• 1 can (15 oz) chickpeas, drained and rinsed
• 1 can (15 oz) diced tomatoes
• Salt and pepper to taste
• Fresh coriander, chopped for garnish
Steps:
Heat olive oil in a large pot. Add onion and garlic, cook until soft.
Stir in cumin, cinnamon, and cayenne. Add sweet potatoes, broth, chickpeas, and tomatoes.
Bring to a boil, then reduce heat to low and simmer for 40 min until sweet potatoes are tender.
Season with salt and pepper. Serve garnished with chopped coriander.
Recommendations:
• Serve with couscous or rice to soak up the delicious flavors.
• Add a squeeze of lemon juice before serving for a fresh flavor contrast.
Nutritional Values: Calories: 260, Fat: 7g, Carbs: 45g, Protein: 8g, Sugar: 13g

CARROT AND GINGER SOUP

PREP: 15 min - **COOKING:** 30 min
MODE OF COOKING: Simmering -
SERVES: 4

Ingr. list:
• 1 Tbsp olive oil
• 1 onion, chopped
• 5 large carrots, peeled and diced
• 2 Tbsp grated fresh ginger
• 4 cups vegetable broth
• Salt and pepper to taste
• Fresh parsley, chopped for garnish
Steps:

Heat olive oil in a large pot over medium heat. Sauté onion until translucent.

Add carrots and ginger, cook for a few minutes until fragrant.

Pour in vegetable broth, bring to a boil then reduce to simmer for 25 minutes or until carrots are very tender.

Blend the soup until smooth using an immersion blender or in batches with a regular blender.

Season with salt and pepper to taste. Serve hot, garnished with fresh parsley.

Recommendations:
• Serve with a swirl of coconut milk for added creaminess and a hint of sweetness.
• A pinch of nutmeg or cinnamon can enhance the warmth of the ginger.
Nutritional Values: Calories: 150, Fat: 5g, Carbs: 25g, Protein: 2g, Sugar: 12g

HEARTY MUSHROOM BARLEY SOUP

PREP: 20 min - **COOKING:** 1 hr
MODE OF COOKING: Simmering - **SERVES:** 6

Ingr. list:
• 1 Tbsp olive oil
• 1 cup chopped onions
• 2 garlic cloves, minced
• 1 cup sliced mushrooms (mix of cremini, shiitake, and button)
• 3/4 cup barley, rinsed
• 6 cups vegetable broth
• 1 tsp dried thyme
• Salt and pepper to taste
• Fresh thyme for garnish
Steps:
Heat olive oil in a large pot over medium heat. Add onions and garlic, cook until onions are softened.

Add mushrooms and cook until they begin to release their juices.

Stir in barley, vegetable broth, and dried thyme. Bring to a boil.

Reduce heat to a simmer, cover, and cook for about 45 minutes or until barley is tender.

Season with salt and pepper to taste. Serve hot, garnished with fresh thyme.

Recommendations:
• Perfect for a cold day, this soup is filling and nutritious.
• Serve with crusty bread for dipping into the savory broth.
Nutritional Values: Calories: 180, Fat: 3g, Carbs: 35g, Protein: 6g, Sugar: 5g

BUTTERNUT SQUASH AND RED LENTIL STEW

PREP: 15 min - **COOKING:** 40 min
MODE OF COOKING: Simmering - **SERVES:** 4

Ingr. list:
• 1 Tbsp olive oil
• 1 onion, diced
• 2 cloves garlic, minced
• 1 small butternut squash, peeled and cubed
• 1 cup red lentils

- 1 quart vegetable broth
- 1 tsp ground cumin
- 1/2 tsp smoked paprika
- Salt and pepper to taste
- Fresh cilantro for garnish

Steps:
Heat olive oil in a large pot over medium heat. Sauté onion and garlic until soft.
Add butternut squash and red lentils, stirring to coat with onion and garlic.
Pour in vegetable broth, add cumin and smoked paprika, and bring to a boil.
Reduce heat and simmer for about 30 minutes or until squash and lentils are tender.
Season with salt and pepper to taste.
Serve hot, garnished with fresh cilantro.

Recommendations:
- Serve this stew over a bed of cooked quinoa or rice for a more substantial meal.
- Add a dollop of plain yogurt or a squeeze of lime for added flavor.

Nutritional Values: Calories: 260, Fat: 4g, Carbs: 50g, Protein: 14g, Sugar: 6g

---

SPICY THAI TEMPEH WRAP

PREP: 20 min - **COOKING:** 10 min
MODE OF COOKING: Sautéing - SERVES: 4

Ingr. list:
- 1 lb (450g) tempeh, sliced into strips
- 2 Tbsp tamari (gluten-free if needed)
- 1 Tbsp sesame oil
- 1 tsp chili flakes
- 1 carrot, julienned
- 1 cucumber, julienned
- 1/4 cup fresh cilantro, chopped
- 4 large whole wheat tortillas or collard greens for a gluten-free option
- 2 Tbsp homemade peanut sauce (blend peanuts with a bit of water, a touch of maple syrup, and a splash of tamari)

Steps:
Marinate tempeh strips in tamari, sesame oil, and chili flakes for 10 min. Sauté tempeh in a non-stick pan over medium heat until golden brown, about 10 min.
Lay tortillas or collard greens flat, spread a thin layer of peanut sauce, then top with sautéed tempeh, carrot, cucumber, and cilantro.
Roll up tightly, slice in half, and serve.

Recommendations:
- Add a squeeze of lime juice to the wrap for extra zest.
- Include additional raw veggies like bell peppers or sprouts for added crunch and nutrients.

Nutritional Values: Calories: 260, Fat: 10g, Carbs: 30g, Protein: 18g, Sugar: 5g

MEDITERRANEAN CHICKPEA SALAD SANDWICH

PREP: 15 min - **COOKING**: 0 min
MODE OF COOKING: Mixing - SERVES: 4

Ingr. list:
- 1 can (15 oz) chickpeas, rinsed and drained
- 1/4 cup red onion, finely chopped
- 1/4 cup kalamata olives, pitted and chopped
- 1/4 cup feta cheese, crumbled
- 2 Tbsp olive oil
- 1 Tbsp lemon juice
- 1/2 tsp dried oregano
- Salt and pepper to taste
- 4 whole wheat pita breads

Steps:
In a bowl, mash chickpeas slightly with a fork, leaving some texture.
Add red onion, olives, feta cheese, olive oil, lemon juice, oregano, salt, and pepper; mix until combined.
Spoon chickpea salad into pita breads and serve.

Recommendations:
- Serve with a side of mixed greens for a complete meal.
- Drizzle a little more olive oil on top for added richness.

Nutritional Values: Calories: 330, Fat: 14g, Carbs: 42g, Protein: 12g, Sugar: 6g

AVOCADO AND HUMMUS VEGGIE WRAP

PREP: 10 min - **COOKING**: 0 min
MODE OF COOKING: Assembling - SERVES: 4

Ingr. list:
- 2 ripe avocados, sliced
- 1 cup hummus
- 1 red bell pepper, thinly sliced
- 1 small red onion, thinly sliced
- 1 cup arugula
- 4 spinach tortillas

Steps:
Spread hummus evenly over each tortilla.

Lay slices of avocado, bell pepper, onion, and a handful of arugula on top of the hummus.
Roll up the tortillas tightly, cut in half, and serve.

Recommendations:
- For an extra protein boost, add a layer of thinly sliced grilled tofu.
- If you like a bit of spice, a few dashes of hot sauce or a sprinkle of crushed red pepper works great.

Nutritional Values: Calories: 320, Fat: 18g, Carbs: 34g, Protein: 9g, Sugar: 4

ROASTED VEGETABLE AND PESTO PANINI

PREP: 15 min - **COOKING:** 20 min
MODE OF COOKING: Roasting/Grilling - **SERVES**: 4

Ingr. list:
- 1 zucchini, sliced lengthwise
- 1 yellow squash, sliced lengthwise
- 1 eggplant, sliced lengthwise
- 2 Tbsp olive oil
- Salt and pepper to taste
- 4 ciabatta rolls, split
- 1/4 cup pesto
- 1/4 cup goat cheese, softened

Steps:
Toss zucchini, squash, and eggplant slices in olive oil, salt, and pepper.
Roast in preheated oven at 425°F (220°C) until tender, about 20 min.
Spread pesto on one side of each ciabatta roll, and goat cheese on the other side.
Layer roasted vegetables between ciabatta rolls. Grill on a panini press until bread is crispy and marks appear, about 5 min.

Recommendations:
- If you don't have a panini press, use a heavy skillet to press the sandwich while grilling.
- Serve with a side salad or soup for a

hearty lunch.
Nutritional Values: Calories: 450, Fat: 22g, Carbs: 52g, Protein: 15g, Sugar: 8g

CURRIED CHICKPEA WRAP

PREP: 15 min - **COOKING**: 10 min
MODE OF COOKING: Sautéing -
SERVES: 4

Ingr. list:
• 1 can (15 oz) chickpeas, drained, rinsed, and lightly mashed
• 1 Tbsp olive oil
• 1 Tbsp curry powder
• 1/2 cup carrots, grated
• 1/2 cup cabbage, shredded
• 1/4 cup raisins
• 4 large whole wheat tortillas or collard greens for a gluten-free option
• 1/4 cup coconut yogurt or other plant-based yogurt
Steps:
Heat olive oil in a pan over medium heat. Add mashed chickpeas and curry powder, sauté until lightly golden, about 10 min.
Remove from heat, stir in carrots, cabbage, and raisins.
Spread plant-based yogurt on each tortilla or collard green leaf, top with the chickpea mixture, roll tightly, slice in half, and serve.
Recommendations:
• Adjust the amount of curry powder based on your spice preference.
• A squeeze of lime juice in the chickpea mixture can add a nice zest to the wrap.
• Add fresh coriander for enhanced flavor and garnish.
Nutritional Values: Calories: 290, Fat: 8g, Carbs: 45g, Protein: 12g, Sugar: 10g

GRILLED PORTOBELLO MUSHROOM SANDWICH

PREP: 15 min - **COOKING:** 10 min
MODE OF COOKING: Grilling -
SERVES: 4

Ingr. list:
• 4 large portobello mushroom caps
• 2 Tbsp balsamic vinegar
• 2 Tbsp olive oil
• 1 garlic clove, minced
• Salt and pepper to taste
• 4 whole wheat buns
• 1/2 cup roasted red peppers
• 1/4 cup pesto
Steps:
Marinate mushroom caps in balsamic vinegar, olive oil, garlic, salt, and pepper for 10 min.
Grill mushrooms over medium heat until tender, about 5 min per side.
Spread pesto on the bottom half of each bun, place a grilled mushroom, top with roasted red peppers, and cover with the top bun.
Recommendations:
• Add a slice of provolone or mozzarella for a cheesy touch.
• Serve with a side of mixed greens for

a complete meal.
Nutritional Values: Calories: 310,
Fat: 16g, Carbs: 34g, Protein: 10g,
Sugar: 8g

Chapter 9: Dinner Recipes

EGGPLANT AND CHICKPEA BAKE

PREP: 20 min - **COOKING**: 40 min
MODE OF COOKING: Baking -
SERVES: 4

Ingr. list:
• 2 medium eggplants, sliced into 1/2-inch rounds
• 1 can (15 oz) chickpeas, drained and rinsed
• 2 cups marinara sauce
• 1 cup vegan mozzarella cheese, shredded
• 1/4 cup fresh basil, chopped
• 2 Tbsp olive oil
• Salt and pepper to taste

Steps:
Preheat oven to 375°F (190°C). Brush eggplant slices with olive oil and season with salt and pepper. Arrange on a baking sheet and roast for 20 min until slightly tender.
In a baking dish, layer roasted eggplant, chickpeas, and marinara sauce. Repeat layers until all ingredients are used.

Top with vegan mozzarella cheese and bake for another 20 min.
Garnish with fresh basil before serving.
Recommendations:
• For added flavor, incorporate a layer of sautéed spinach or mushrooms between the eggplant slices.
• Allow the bake to rest for 10 min before serving to help set the layers.
Nutritional Values: Calories: 320, Fat: 15g, Carbs: 38g, Protein: 12g, Sugar: 13g

SWEET POTATO AND BLACK BEAN CASSEROLE

PREP: 15 min - **COOKING**: 45 min
MODE OF COOKING: Baking -
SERVES: 6

Ingr. list:
• 3 large sweet potatoes, peeled and cubed
• 1 can (15 oz) black beans, drained and rinsed
• 1 red bell pepper, diced
• 1 green bell pepper, diced
• 1 onion, chopped
• 2 cloves garlic, minced
• 1 tsp cumin
• 1 tsp chili powder
• 1/2 tsp smoked paprika
• 1 cup shredded vegan cheddar cheese
• 2 Tbsp olive oil
• Salt and pepper to taste
Steps:
Preheat oven to 375°F (190°C). Toss sweet potatoes with olive oil, cumin, chili powder, smoked paprika, salt, and pepper. Spread on a baking tray and roast for 25 min until tender.
In a skillet, sauté onion, garlic, and bell peppers until softened, about 10 min.
In a large casserole dish, layer roasted sweet potatoes, sautéed vegetables, and black beans. Top with vegan cheddar cheese.

Bake for 20 min or until the cheese is melted and bubbly.

Recommendations:
• Serve with a dollop of vegan sour cream or a drizzle of avocado cream for added richness.
• Sprinkle with fresh cilantro for a burst of flavor before serving.

Nutritional Values: Calories: 290, Fat: 9g, Carbs: 44g, Protein: 10g, Sugar: 9g

MUSHROOM AND KALE STRATA

PREP: 30 min - **COOKING:** 35 min
MODE OF COOKING: Baking -
SERVES: 4

Ingr. list:
• 1 lb. mushrooms, sliced
• 4 cups kale, chopped and stemmed
• 6 slices whole grain bread, cubed
• 1 cup unsweetened almond milk
• 3 Tbsp nutritional yeast
• 1 tsp thyme
• 1 tsp garlic powder
• 1/2 tsp salt
• 1/4 tsp black pepper
• 2 Tbsp olive oil

Steps:
Preheat oven to 350°F (177°C). Sauté mushrooms in olive oil until golden, about 10 min. Add kale and cook until wilted.
In a bowl, whisk together almond milk, nutritional yeast, thyme, garlic powder, salt, and pepper.
In a greased baking dish, layer half the bread cubes, then top with half the mushroom and kale mixture. Repeat layers. Pour the almond milk mixture evenly over the top.
Bake for 35 min or until the top is golden and crisp.

Recommendations:
• For a richer flavor, add a splash of white wine to the mushrooms while cooking.
• Let the strata sit for 10 min after baking for easier serving.

Nutritional Values: Calories: 330, Fat: 14g, Carbs: 40g, Protein: 12g, Sugar: 6g

SPINACH AND MUSHROOM LASAGNA

PREP: 30 min - **COOKING**: 45 min
MODE OF COOKING: Baking -
SERVES: 6

Ingr. list:
• 9 no-boil lasagna noodles
• 3 cups fresh spinach, chopped
• 2 cups mushrooms, sliced
• 1 onion, diced
• 3 cloves garlic, minced
• 1 can (15 oz) crushed tomatoes
• 1 cup ricotta cheese, vegan
• 1 cup mozzarella cheese, vegan, shredded
• 2 Tbsp olive oil
• 1 tsp dried basil
• 1 tsp dried oregano
• Salt and pepper to taste

Steps:
Preheat oven to 375°F (190°C). In a skillet, heat olive oil over medium heat. Sauté onion, garlic, mushrooms until softened, about 8 min.
Add spinach and cook until wilted. Stir in crushed tomatoes, basil, oregano, salt, and pepper. Simmer for 10 min.
In a baking dish, layer lasagna noodles, spinach-mushroom sauce, and dollops of ricotta. Repeat layers, ending with noodles topped with mozzarella.
Cover with foil and bake for 35 min. Remove foil and bake for an additional 10 min until cheese is bubbly and golden.

Recommendations:
• Let the lasagna sit for 10 min before slicing to help it set.

• Enhance the dish with a sprinkle of nutritional yeast for added flavor and vitamins.
Nutritional Values: Calories: 310, Fat: 14g, Carbs: 34g, Protein: 16g, Sugar: 5g

RATATOUILLE BAKED ZITI

PREP: 25 min - **COOKING**: 30 min
MODE OF COOKING: Baking -
SERVES: 6

Ingr. list:
• 2 zucchinis, diced
• 1 eggplant, diced
• 1 red bell pepper, diced
• 1 yellow bell pepper, diced
• 1 onion, diced
• 3 cloves garlic, minced
• 2 cups marinara sauce
• 1/2 cup basil leaves, chopped
• 12 oz. ziti pasta, cooked al dente
• 1 cup vegan parmesan cheese, grated
• 3 Tbsp olive oil
• Salt and pepper to taste

Steps:
Preheat oven to 375°F (190°C). In a large pan, heat olive oil over medium heat. Sauté zucchini, eggplant, bell peppers, onion, and garlic until softened, about 10 min.
Stir in marinara sauce and basil. Simmer for 5 min, then mix with cooked pasta.
Transfer to a baking dish, sprinkle with vegan parmesan. Bake uncovered for 30 min until the top is crispy and browned.

Recommendations:
• Serve with a side of garlic bread or a simple green salad for a complete meal.
• Add chili flakes for a spicy kick if desired.
Nutritional Values: Calories: 360, Fat: 12g, Carbs: 52g, Protein: 12g, Sugar: 8g

SWEET POTATO SHEPHERD'S PIE

PREP: 20 min - **COOKING**: 40 min
MODE OF COOKING: Baking -
SERVES: 6

Ingr. list:
• 4 large sweet potatoes, peeled and cubed
• 1 lb. lentils, cooked
• 1 carrot, diced
• 1 celery stalk, diced
• 1 onion, diced
• 2 cloves garlic, minced
• 1 cup vegetable broth
• 1/2 cup almond milk
• 2 Tbsp olive oil
• 1 tsp thyme
• Salt and pepper to taste

Steps:
Preheat oven to 400°F (204°C). Boil sweet potatoes until tender, about 15 min. Drain and mash with almond milk, salt, and pepper.
In a skillet, heat olive oil over medium heat. Sauté onion, garlic, carrot, and celery until softened. Add lentils, vegetable broth, and thyme. Simmer until thickened, about 10 min.
Layer lentil mixture in a baking dish, then top with mashed sweet potatoes. Bake for 20 min or until the top is slightly crispy.

Recommendations:
• For a richer flavor, add a splash of red wine to the lentil mixture during cooking.
• Garnish with fresh parsley for color and freshness before serving.
Nutritional Values: Calories: 390, Fat: 9g, Carbs: 62g, Protein: 18g, Sugar: 11g

THAI TEMPEH AND BASIL STIR-FRY

PREP: 15 min - **COOKING:** 10 min

MODE OF COOKING: Stir-frying - **SERVES:** 4

Ingr. list:
- 14 oz. tempeh, cut into cubes
- 2 cups Thai basil leaves
- 1 red bell pepper, sliced
- 1 yellow bell pepper, sliced
- 2 cloves garlic, minced
- 2 Tbsp tamari (or soy sauce if not avoiding all processed ingredients)
- 1 Tbsp sesame oil
- 1 tsp chili paste (ensure it's free from additives)
- 1 Tbsp ginger, grated
- 1 Tbsp peanut oil

Steps:
Heat peanut oil in a large skillet over medium-high heat. Add tempeh cubes and stir-fry until golden brown, about 5 min.

Add garlic, ginger, and bell peppers to the skillet. Stir-fry for another 3 min.

Lower the heat, then add tamari, sesame oil, and chili paste, stirring to coat evenly.

Stir in Thai basil leaves just before removing from heat to preserve their flavor and color.

Recommendations:
- Serve hot over a bed of jasmine rice or whole grain rice for a complete meal.
- Adjust the amount of chili paste based on your preference for spice. Fresh chili can also be used for a more natural spice source.

Nutritional Values: Calories: 220, Fat: 12g, Carbs: 12g, Protein: 16g, Sugar: 4g

COCONUT CURRY MEDLEY

PREP: 20 min - **COOKING:** 20 min
MODE OF COOKING: Simmering - **SERVES:** 4

Ingr. list:
- 1 can (14 oz) coconut milk
- 2 carrots, sliced
- 1 sweet potato, cubed
- 1 zucchini, sliced
- 1 broccoli head, cut into florets
- 1 onion, diced
- 2 cloves garlic, minced
- 1 Tbsp curry powder
- 1 tsp turmeric
- 1 Tbsp coconut oil
- Salt to taste

Steps:
Heat coconut oil in a large pot over medium heat. Add onion and garlic, sauté until translucent.

Stir in curry powder and turmeric, cook for 1 min until fragrant.

Add coconut milk, carrots, sweet potato, and bring to a simmer. Cover and cook for 10 min.

Add zucchini and broccoli, continue to simmer uncovered for another 10 min.

Recommendations:

- Serve with a scoop of brown rice or quinoa for a hearty dish.
- Garnish with fresh cilantro or a squeeze of lime juice for extra freshness.

Nutritional Values: Calories: 220, Fat: 14g, Carbs: 22g, Protein: 5g, Sugar: 7g

SZECHUAN EGGPLANT AND MUSHROOM STIR-FRY

PREP: 15 min - **COOKING:** 15 min
MODE OF COOKING: Stir-frying -
SERVES: 4

Ingr. list:
- 2 medium eggplants, cubed
- 1 cup shiitake mushrooms, sliced
- 1 bell pepper, julienned
- 2 Tbsp hoisin sauce
- 1 Tbsp soy sauce
- 2 tsp chili garlic sauce
- 1 tsp sesame oil
- 2 Tbsp vegetable oil
- 2 green onions, chopped
- 1 tsp Szechuan peppercorns, crushed

Steps:
Heat vegetable oil in a large wok over high heat. Add eggplant and stir-fry until browned, about 5 min.
Add mushrooms and bell pepper, continue to stir-fry for 5 more min.
Reduce heat to medium. Stir in hoisin sauce, soy sauce, chili garlic sauce, and sesame oil. Mix well.
Sprinkle with green onions and Szechuan peppercorns before serving.

Recommendations:
- Serve hot with steamed rice or noodles.
- For added crunch, top with toasted sesame seeds.

Nutritional Values: Calories: 180, Fat: 10g, Carbs: 20g, Protein: 4g, Sugar: 9g

LEMONGRASS TEMPEH STIR-FRY

PREP: 15 min - **COOKING:** 10 min
MODE OF COOKING: Stir-frying -
SERVES: 4

Ingr. list:
14 oz. tempeh, pressed and cubed
2 stalks lemongrass, tender inner part finely chopped
1 red bell pepper, julienned
1 green bell pepper, julienned
1 onion, sliced
2 carrots, julienned
3 Tbsp tamari (a gluten-free alternative to soy sauce)
2 Tbsp sesame oil (a healthier choice over vegetable oil)
1 Tbsp ginger, grated
2 cloves garlic, minced
1 tsp chili flakes (optional)

Steps:
Heat sesame oil in a large skillet or wok over medium-high heat. Add tempeh and stir-fry until golden brown, about 5 min. Remove tempeh and set aside.
In the same skillet, add more oil if needed, and sauté garlic, ginger, and lemongrass until fragrant, about 1 min.
Add onions, bell peppers, and carrots to the skillet. Stir-fry until vegetables are just tender, about 5 min.
Return tempeh to the skillet, add tamari and chili flakes if using. Stir well to combine and heat through for another 2 min.

Recommendations:
Serve with jasmine rice or over whole grain noodles for a complete meal.
Garnish with fresh cilantro and a squeeze of lime juice for added freshness.

Nutritional Values: Calories: 220, Fat: 12g, Carbs: 15g, Protein: 18g, Sugar: 5g

RED LENTIL AND SPINACH CURRY

PREP: 10 min - **COOKING:** 20 min
MODE OF COOKING: Simmering -
SERVES: 4

Ingr. list:
1 cup red lentils
4 cups fresh spinach, roughly chopped
1 onion, finely chopped
2 tomatoes, diced
1 can (14 oz) coconut milk
2 Tbsp curry paste
1 Tbsp olive oil
1 tsp turmeric
1 tsp cumin
Salt to taste

Steps:
Heat olive oil in a large saucepan over medium heat. Sauté onion until translucent, about 5 min.
Stir in curry paste, turmeric, and cumin, cook for 1 min until fragrant.
Add red lentils, tomatoes, and coconut milk. Bring to a boil, then reduce heat and simmer until lentils are soft, about 15 min.
Stir in spinach and cook until wilted, about 2 min. Adjust seasoning with salt.

Recommendations:
Serve hot with naan bread or basmati rice for a hearty meal.
Add a dollop of yogurt or a sprinkle of fresh cilantro for extra flavor.

Nutritional Values: Calories: 295, Fat: 15g, Carbs: 29g, Protein: 12g, Sugar: 3g

SPICY BROCCOLI AND PEANUT STIR-FRY

PREP: 10 min - **COOKING:** 10 min
MODE OF COOKING: Stir-frying -
SERVES: 4
Ingr. list:
- 4 cups broccoli florets
- 1 bell pepper, sliced
- 1 onion, sliced
- 1/2 cup roasted peanuts
- 3 Tbsp soy sauce
- 2 Tbsp peanut butter
- 2 Tbsp vegetable oil
- 1 Tbsp honey
- 1 tsp crushed red pepper flakes
- 2 cloves garlic, minced

Steps:
Heat vegetable oil in a large skillet or wok over medium-high heat. Add garlic and stir-fry until fragrant, about 30 sec. Add broccoli, bell pepper, and onion. Stir-fry until vegetables are tender but still crisp, about 7 min.
In a small bowl, whisk together soy sauce, peanut butter, honey, and red pepper flakes until smooth.

Pour sauce over the vegetables, add peanuts, and toss to coat evenly. Cook for another 2 min.
Recommendations:
Excellent when served over steamed rice or noodles.
Adjust the amount of red pepper flakes to suit your taste for spice.
Nutritional Values: Calories: 260, Fat: 18g, Carbs: 18g, Protein: 9g, Sugar: 7g

MOROCCAN QUINOA AND CHICKPEA BOWL

PREP: 15 min - **COOKING:** 20 min
MODE OF COOKING: Simmering - **SERVES:** 4
Ingr. list:
- 1 cup quinoa, rinsed
- 1 can (15 oz) chickpeas, drained and rinsed
- 2 cups vegetable broth
- 1 red bell pepper, diced
- 1/2 cup dried apricots, chopped
- 1/4 cup almonds, sliced
- 2 Tbsp olive oil
- 1 tsp cumin
- 1 tsp coriander
- 1/2 tsp cinnamon
- Salt and pepper to taste

Steps:
In a saucepan, bring vegetable broth to a boil. Add quinoa, cover, and simmer for 15 min until liquid is absorbed.
In a skillet, heat olive oil over medium heat. Sauté bell pepper, cumin, coriander, and cinnamon for 5 min until softened.
Stir in chickpeas, apricots, and cooked quinoa, cook for another 5 min.
Serve hot, garnished with sliced almonds.
Recommendations:
Add a dollop of yogurt or drizzle with tahini for extra creaminess and flavor.

Garnish with fresh cilantro or mint for a burst of freshness.
N.V.: Calories: 320, Fat: 10g, Carbs: 48g, Protein: 12g, Sugar: 12g

ASIAN BROWN RICE AND EDAMAME BOWL

PREP: 10 min - **COOKING:** 30 min
MODE OF COOKING: Boiling - **SERVES:** 4
Ingr. list:
- 1 cup brown rice
- 1 cup edamame, shelled
- 1 carrot, julienned
- 1 cucumber, thinly sliced
- 1/4 cup soy sauce
- 2 Tbsp rice vinegar
- 1 Tbsp sesame oil
- 1 tsp ginger, grated
- 1 clove garlic, minced
- 2 green onions, chopped
- 1 Tbsp sesame seeds

Steps:
Cook brown rice in 2 cups of water for about 30 min until tender.
Steam edamame for 5 min until heated through.
In a small bowl, mix soy sauce, rice vinegar, sesame oil, ginger, and garlic.
Toss cooked rice with vegetables and edamame. Drizzle dressing over the top and mix well.
Garnish with green onions and sesame seeds before serving.
Recommendations:
Perfect as a light lunch or as a side dish with grilled tofu or tempeh.
Add chili flakes or wasabi for an extra kick.
N.V.: Calories: 280, Fat: 8g, Carbs: 42g, Protein: 10g, Sugar: 3g

SWEET POTATO AND BLACK BEAN BURRITO BOWL

PREP: 20 min - **COOKING:** 30 min
MODE OF COOKING: Roasting/Baking
- **SERVES:** 4

Ingr. list:
- 2 large sweet potatoes, peeled and cubed
- 1 can (15 oz) black beans, drained and rinsed
- 1 avocado, diced
- 1 cup corn kernels
- 1/2 red onion, diced
- 1 lime, juiced
- 2 Tbsp olive oil
- 1 tsp chili powder
- 1/2 tsp cumin
- 1/4 cup fresh cilantro, chopped
- Salt and pepper to taste

Steps:
Preheat oven to 400°F (204°C). Toss sweet potatoes with 1 Tbsp olive oil, chili powder, cumin, salt, and pepper. Roast for 25 min until tender.
Combine black beans, corn, red onion, and cilantro in a bowl. Add lime juice and remaining olive oil.
Assemble bowls with a base of roasted sweet potatoes, topped with the black bean mixture and diced avocado.

Recommendations:
Serve with a side of salsa or a dollop of guacamole for extra flavor.
Sprinkle with shredded cheese or a scoop of sour cream if not vegan.

N.V.: Calories: 350, Fat: 14g, Carbs: 52g, Protein: 10g, Sugar: 7g

MEDITERRANEAN FARRO AND CHICKPEA BOWL

PREP: 15 min - **COOKING:** 30 min
MODE OF COOKING: Boiling -
SERVES: 4

Ingr. list:
- 1 cup farro
- 1 can (15 oz) chickpeas, drained and rinsed
- 1 cup cherry tomatoes, halved
- 1 cucumber, diced
- 1/2 red onion, thinly sliced
- 1/4 cup kalamata olives, pitted and halved
- 1/4 cup vegan feta cheese, crumbled
- 1/4 cup parsley, chopped
- 3 Tbsp olive oil
- 2 Tbsp lemon juice
- 1 tsp dried oregano
- Salt and pepper to taste

Steps:
Cook farro in boiling water according to package instructions until tender, about 30 min; drain well.

In a large bowl, combine cooked farro, chickpeas, cherry tomatoes, cucumber, red onion, olives, and parsley.

Whisk together olive oil, lemon juice, oregano, salt, and pepper. Drizzle over the salad and toss to combine. Sprinkle with vegan feta cheese before serving.

Recommendations: Chill the salad for at least an hour before serving to enhance the flavors. Serve as a standalone meal or pair with grilled vegetables for added variety.

N.V.: Calories: 340, Fat: 14g, Carbs: 45g, Protein: 12g, Sugar: 5g

CURRIED LENTIL AND WILD RICE BOWL

PREP: 10 min - **COOKING:** 45 min
MODE OF COOKING: Simmering - **SERVES:** 4

Ingr. list:
- 1/2 cup wild rice
- 1/2 cup brown lentils
- 1 carrot, diced
- 1 bell pepper, diced
- 1 small sweet potato, cubed
- 4 cups vegetable broth
- 2 tsp curry powder
- 1 tsp turmeric
- 1 tsp cumin
- 1/2 tsp cinnamon
- Salt to taste
- Fresh cilantro, for garnish

Steps: Rinse wild rice and lentils under cold water until water runs clear. In a large pot, combine wild rice, lentils, carrot, bell pepper, sweet potato, and vegetable broth. Bring to a boil. Reduce heat to a simmer, add curry powder, turmeric, cumin, and cinnamon. Cover and cook until the lentils and rice are tender, about 45 min. Season with salt, and garnish with fresh cilantro before serving.

Recommendations: Serve with a side of naan bread or pita for a hearty meal. Add a spoonful of yogurt or a squeeze of lime for a creamy texture and a tang of brightness.

N.V.: Calories: 255, Fat: 1.5g, Carbs: 50g, Protein: 12g, Sugar: 5g

ROASTED VEGETABLE AND BARLEY BOWL

PREP: 20 min - **COOKING:** 40 min
MODE OF COOKING: Roasting and boiling - **SERVES:** 4

Ingr. list:
- 1 cup barley
- 1 zucchini, cubed
- 1 red bell pepper, cubed
- 1 yellow squash, cubed
- 1 red onion, chopped
- 2 Tbsp olive oil
- 1 tsp smoked paprika
- Salt and pepper to taste
- 1/4 cup toasted almonds, chopped
- 1/4 cup basil, chiffonade

Steps: Preheat oven to 400°F (204°C). Toss zucchini, bell pepper, yellow squash, and red onion with olive oil, smoked paprika, salt, and pepper. Spread on a baking sheet and roast until vegetables are tender, about 25 min. Meanwhile, cook barley in boiling water until tender, about 30 min; drain. Combine roasted vegetables with cooked barley in a large bowl. Adjust seasoning if necessary. Garnish with toasted almonds and basil before serving.

Recommendations: For a protein boost, add chickpeas or black beans to the mix. Drizzle with a balsamic reduction for added depth of flavor.

N.V.: Calories: 340, Fat: 10g, Carbs: 55g, Protein: 9g, Sugar: 6g

Chapter 10: Snack and Appetizer

ROASTED RED PEPPER HUMMUS

PREP: 10 min - **COOKING:** 0 min
MODE OF COOKING: Blending -
SERVES: 6
Ingr. list:
- 1 can (15 oz) chickpeas, drained and rinsed
- 1 cup roasted red peppers, drained
- 2 Tbsp tahini
- 2 cloves garlic, minced
- 2 Tbsp lemon juice
- 2 Tbsp olive oil
- 1 tsp smoked paprika
- Salt and pepper to taste

Steps: Combine chickpeas, roasted red peppers, tahini, garlic, lemon juice, olive oil, and smoked paprika in a food processor. Blend until smooth. Season with salt and pepper to taste. Transfer to a serving bowl and sprinkle with olive oil before serving. Garnish with chopped parsley or a sprinkle of sesame seeds for extra texture and flavour. Serve with pita chips, veggie sticks, or as a spread for sandwiches.
N.V.: Calories: 150, Fat: 8g, Carbs: 15g, Protein: 5g, Sugar: 2g

AVOCADO AND EDAMAME DIP

PREP: 15 min - **COOKING:** 0 min
MODE OF COOKING: Blending -
SERVES: 4
Ingr. list:
- 1 cup edamame, shelled and cooked
- 1 ripe avocado, peeled and pitted
- 1 small onion, chopped
- 1 clove garlic, minced
- 2 Tbsp lime juice
- 1/4 cup cilantro, chopped
- Salt and chili flakes to taste

Steps: In a food processor, blend edamame, avocado, onion, garlic, lime juice, and cilantro until smooth. Season with salt and chili flakes according to taste. Chill in the refrigerator for at least 30 minutes before serving to enhance the flavors.
Recommendations: Perfect as a dip for tortilla chips or crudité. Can also be used as a flavourful spread on wraps or veggie burgers.
N.V.: Calories: 180, Fat: 12g, Carbs: 12g, Protein: 7g, Sugar: 2g

SUN-DRIED TOMATO AND WHITE BEAN DIP

PREP: 10 min - **COOKING:** 0 min
MODE OF COOKING: Blending -
SERVES: 6
Ingr. list:
- 1 can (15 oz) white beans, drained and rinsed
- 1/2 cup sun-dried tomatoes, oil-packed, drained

- 2 Tbsp olive oil
- 2 cloves garlic, minced
- 1 Tbsp lemon juice
- 1 tsp dried basil
- Salt and pepper to taste

Steps: Combine white beans, sun-dried tomatoes, olive oil, garlic, lemon juice, and dried basil in a food processor. Blend until the mixture is smooth and creamy. Add salt and pepper to taste. Pour the blend into a serving bowl and let it rest for a few minutes to enhance the flavors.

Recommendations: Garnish with a drizzle of olive oil and some chopped fresh basil or chives for a fresh touch. Serve with warm crusty bread, crackers, or as a sandwich spread.

N.V.: Calories: 130, Fat: 5g, Carbs: 17g, Protein: 6g, Sugar: 2g

CREAMY BEET AND WALNUT DIP

PREP: 15 min - **COOKING:** 0 min
MODE OF COOKING: Blending -
SERVES: 4

Ingr. list:
- 2 medium beets, cooked and peeled
- 1/2 cup walnuts, toasted
- 2 Tbsp tahini
- 2 cloves garlic, minced
- 2 Tbsp lemon juice
- 1 Tbsp olive oil
- Salt and pepper to taste

Steps: Chop the cooked beets into chunks and place them in a food processor with the toasted walnuts, tahini, garlic, and lemon juice. Blend until smooth, drizzling in olive oil while the processor runs. Season with salt and pepper, adjusting to taste.

Recommendations: Serve chilled with a garnish of chopped chives or dill for added flavor and color. Perfect as a

vibrant spread on crackers or as a dip for fresh vegetable sticks.

N.V.: Calories: 220, Fat: 15g, Carbs: 18g, Protein: 6g, Sugar: 8g

SPICY BLACK BEAN AND CORN DIP

PREP: 10 min - **COOKING:** 0 min
MODE OF COOKING: Mixing -
SERVES: 6

Ingr. list:
- 1 can (15 oz) black beans, drained and rinsed
- 1 cup corn kernels, fresh or thawed if frozen
- 1/2 red bell pepper, finely chopped
- 1 jalapeño, seeded and minced
- 1/4 cup red onion, finely chopped
- 2 Tbsp cilantro, chopped
- 2 Tbsp lime juice
- 1 Tbsp olive oil
- Salt and chili powder to taste

Steps: In a mixing bowl, combine black beans, corn, red bell pepper, jalapeño, and red onion. Combine cilantro, lime juice, and olive oil. Toss everything until thoroughly combined. Season with salt and chilli powder to taste.

Recommendation: To enhance the flavours, chill the dip for an hour before serving. Serve with Mexican chips or as a stuffing in quesadillas or burritos.

N.V.: Calories: 140, Fat: 3g, Carbs: 23g, Protein: 7g, Sugar: 2g

HERBED YOGURT AND CUCUMBER DIP

PREP: 15 min - **COOKING:** 0 min
MODE OF COOKING: Mixing -
SERVES: 4

Ingr. list:

- 1 cup plain Greek yogurt, vegan
- 1 cucumber, seeded and finely diced
- 2 Tbsp mint, finely chopped
- 2 Tbsp dill, finely chopped
- 1 clove garlic, minced
- 2 Tbsp lemon juice
- Salt and pepper to taste

Steps: Combine all ingredients in a bowl and mix well until fully integrated. Chill in the refrigerator for at least 30 minutes to allow flavours to combine.
Recommendations: Serve with pita bread, fresh vegetables, or as a cooling side to spicy dishes. Add a drizzle of olive oil over the top before serving for an extra touch of richness.
N.V.: Calories: 70, Fat: 1g, Carbs: 8g, Protein: 6g, Sugar: 5g

CRISPY KALE CHIPS

PREP: 10 min - **COOKING:** 15 min
MODE OF COOKING: Baking -
SERVES: 4

Ingr. list:
- 1 bunch kale, stems removed and leaves torn
- 1 Tbsp olive oil
- 1/4 tsp salt
- 1/4 tsp garlic powder

Steps: Preheat oven to 350°F (175°C). Wash the kale and ensure it is completely dry using a salad spinner or paper towels. In a large bowl, mix the kale with olive oil, salt, and garlic powder, making sure it's evenly coated. Arrange the kale in a single layer on a baking sheet. Bake for 15 min, turning halfway through, until crisp.
Suggestions: Keep a vigilant eye on the kale chips while baking, as they can quickly transition from perfectly crispy to burnt. Experiment with other seasonings like smoked paprika or nutritional yeast for variety.

N.V.: Calories: 58, Fat: 3.5g, Carbs: 6g, Protein: 2g, Sugar: 1g

BAKED ZUCCHINI FRIES

PREP: 15 min - **COOKING:** 20 min
MODE OF COOKING: Baking -
SERVES: 4

Ingr. list:
- 4 medium zucchinis, cut into 3-inch sticks
- 1/2 cup almond flour
- 1/4 cup ground flaxseed
- 1 tsp Italian seasoning
- 1/2 tsp salt
- 1/4 tsp black pepper
- 1/4 cup unsweetened almond milk

Steps: Preheat oven to 425°F (220°C). Place parchment paper on a baking sheet. In a bowl, mix together almond flour, ground flaxseed, Italian seasoning, salt, and pepper. Submerge the zucchini sticks in almond milk, then roll them in the flour mixture until fully coated. Place on the prepared baking sheet and bake for 20 min, turning halfway through, until golden and crispy.
Recommendations: Serve with a side of marinara sauce for dipping. Make sure zucchini sticks are dry before coating to help the breading stick.
N.V.: Calories: 120, Fat: 7g, Carbs: 10g, Protein: 5g, Sugar: 3g

SWEET POTATO AND BEET CHIPS

PREP: 15 min - **COOKING:** 25 min
MODE OF COOKING: Baking -
SERVES: 4

Ingr. list:
- 2 large sweet potatoes, thinly sliced

- 2 large beets, thinly sliced
- 2 Tbsp olive oil
- 1/2 tsp sea salt
- 1/4 tsp ground black pepper

Steps: Preheat oven to 375°F (190°C). Line two baking sheets with parchment paper. In separate bowls, toss sweet potato slices and beet slices with olive oil, salt, and pepper. Spread slices in a single layer on the baking sheets, ensuring they don't overlap. Bake for 25 min, flipping once halfway through, until crisp and slightly browned.

Recommendations: Use a mandoline for evenly thin slices, which helps them crisp up better. Keep an eye on the chips, as cooking times may vary based on thickness and oven performance.

N.V.: Calories: 140, Fat: 7g, Carbs: 18g, Protein: 2g, Sugar: 5g

SPICED CHICKPEA CRUNCHIES

PREP: 5 min - **COOKING:** 30 min
MODE OF COOKING: Roasting -
SERVES: 4

Ingr. list:

- 1 can (15 oz) chickpeas, drained, rinsed, and dried
- 1 Tbsp olive oil
- 1 tsp smoked paprika
- 1/2 tsp cumin
- 1/4 tsp chili powder
- 1/4 tsp garlic powder
- Salt to taste

Steps: Preheat oven to 400°F (204°C). In a bowl, toss chickpeas with olive oil, smoked papapa, cumin, chili powder, garlic powder, and salt. Spread chickpeas in a single layer on a baking sheet. Roast for 30 min, shaking the pan halfway through, until crisp and golden.

Recommendations: Let cool completely before serving to enhance the crunch. Store in an airtight container to maintain freshness.

N.V.: Calories: 134, Fat: 5g, Carbs: 18g, Protein: 6g, Sugar: 0g

PARMESAN CAULIFLOWER POPPERS

PREP: 10 min - **COOKING:** 20 min
MODE OF COOKING: Baking -
SERVES: 4
Ingr. list:

- 1 large cauliflower, cut into bite-sized florets
- 1/4 cup grated Parmesan cheese, vegan
- 1 Tbsp olive oil
- 1/2 tsp garlic powder
- 1/2 tsp onion powder
- Salt and pepper to taste

Steps: Preheat oven to 425°F (220°C). In a large bowl, toss cauliflower florets with olive oil, garlic powder, onion powder, salt, and pepper. Sprinkle with vegan Parmesan cheese and toss again until evenly coated. Spread cauliflower on a baking sheet in a single layer. Bake for 20 min, turning halfway through, until golden and crispy.

Recommendations: Serve with a side of marinara sauce for dipping. For an extra kick, add a pinch of red pepper flakes before baking.
N.V.: Calories: 98, Fat: 5g, Carbs: 10g, Protein: 4g, Sugar: 3g

CURRIED PEANUT AND SWEET POTATO BALLS

PREP: 15 min - **COOKING:** 25 min
MODE OF COOKING: Baking -
SERVES: 4

Ingr. list:
- 2 large sweet potatoes, cooked and mashed
- 1/2 cup peanuts, finely chopped
- 1 Tbsp curry powder
- 1 tsp ginger, grated
- 1/2 tsp salt
- 2 Tbsp coconut oil

Steps: Preheat oven to 375°F (190°C). In a bowl, mix mashed sweet potatoes, chopped peanuts, curry powder, ginger, and salt. Form mixture into small balls, about the size of a golf ball. Place balls on a baking sheet greased with coconut oil. Bake for 25 min, turning halfway through, until the outside is crispy and golden.
Recommendations: Serve hot, garnished with cilantro or a dollop of coconut yogurt for a cooling contrast. These are perfect as a party appetizer or as a savory snack on the go.
N.V.: Calories: 160, Fat: 9g, Carbs: 18g, Protein: 4g, Sugar: 5g

ALMOND AND CHIA ENERGY BITES

PREP: 15 min - **COOKING:** 0 min
MODE OF COOKING: No cook -
SERVES: 12

Ingr. list:

- 1 cup rolled oats
- 1/2 cup almond butter
- 1/4 cup chia seeds
- 1/4 cup flaxseed meal
- 1/3 cup maple syrup
- 1 tsp vanilla extract
- 1/2 tsp cinnamon
- Pinch of salt

Steps: In a large bowl, mix together oats, almond butter, chia seeds, flaxseed meal, maple syrup, vanilla extract, cinnamon, and salt until well combined. Chill the mixture in the refrigerator for 10 min to make it easier to handle. Roll the mixture into balls, about 1 inch in diameter.
Recommendations: Store in an airtight container in the refrigerator for up to a week. For added texture, roll the bites in crushed almonds or coconut flakes before chilling.
N.V.: Calories: 150, Fat: 8g, Carbs: 16g, Protein: 4g, Sugar: 7g

PUMPKIN SPICE ENERGY BALLS

PREP: 20 min - **COOKING:** 0 min
MODE OF COOKING: No cook -
SERVES: 15

Ingr. list:
- 1 cup pitted dates
- 1/2 cup raw pecans
- 1/3 cup pumpkin puree
- 3/4 cup rolled oats
- 1/4 cup hemp seeds
- 2 tsp pumpkin pie spice
- 1/4 tsp salt
- 1 Tbsp maple syrup

Steps: Place dates and pecans in a food processor and pulse until finely chopped and mixed. Add pumpkin puree, oats, hemp seeds, pumpkin pie spice, salt, and maple syrup. Pulse until the mixture is well combined and sticks together. Roll the mixture into balls, about 1 inch in diameter.

Recommendations: Chill the balls for at least an hour before serving to help them set. Dust with extra pumpkin pie spice or cocoa powder for a decorative finish.

N.V.: Calories: 100, Fat: 5g, Carbs: 13g, Protein: 3g, Sugar: 8g

COCOA AND WALNUT ENERGY BITES

PREP: 15 min - **COOKING:** 0 min
MODE OF COOKING: No cook -
SERVES: 10
Ingr. list:
- 1 cup walnuts
- 1 cup medjool dates, pitted
- 1/4 cup cocoa powder
- 1/2 tsp vanilla extract
- Pinch of salt
- 2 Tbsp coconut oil, melted

Steps: In a food processor, combine walnuts and dates until they form a sticky mixture. Add cocoa powder, vanilla extract, salt, and coconut oil. Process until the mixture is smooth and holds together. Roll the mixture into balls, about 1 inch in diameter.

Recommendations: For an extra crunch, roll the bites in crushed nuts or cocoa nibs. Keep these bites refrigerated in an airtight container to maintain freshness.

N.V.: Calories: 180, Fat: 10g, Carbs: 22g, Protein: 3g, Sugar: 18g

MATCHA GREEN TEA ENERGY BALLS

PREP: 15 min - **COOKING:** 0 min
MODE OF COOKING: No cook -
SERVES: 12

Ingr. list:
- 1 cup cashews
- 1/2 cup shredded unsweetened coconut
- 1/4 cup hemp seeds
- 2 Tbsp matcha green tea powder
- 1/4 cup honey (or agave syrup for vegan option)
- 1 tsp vanilla extract
- Pinch of salt

Steps: Place cashews, coconut, and hemp seeds in a food processor and blend until finely ground. Add matcha powder, honey, vanilla extract, and a pinch of salt. Process until the mixture sticks together and forms a dough-like consistency. Roll the mixture into balls, about 1 inch in diameter, and coat with extra shredded coconut if desired.

Recommendations: Refrigerate for 30 minutes before serving to allow the flavors to meld and the texture to firm up. These can be stored in the refrigerator for up to a week or frozen for longer storage.

N.V.: Calories: 140, Fat: 9g, Carbs: 12g, Protein: 4g, Sugar: 7g

LEMON TURMERIC ENERGY BALLS

PREP: 15 min - **COOKING:** 0 min
MODE OF COOKING: No cook -
SERVES: 10
Ingr. list:
- 1 cup raw almonds
- 1 cup pitted dates
- 2 Tbsp lemon zest
- 1 Tbsp lemon juice
- 1 tsp turmeric powder
- 1/4 tsp black pepper
- 2 Tbsp chia seeds

Steps: Combine almonds and dates in a food processor until they form a coarse paste. Add lemon zest, lemon juice, turmeric powder, black pepper, and chia seeds to the paste and blend until the mixture becomes uniform and sticky. Roll the mixture into balls, about 1 inch in diameter, and optionally coat with extra chia seeds or shredded coconut.

Recommendations: The black pepper enhances the absorption of curcumin from turmeric, increasing its health benefits. Keep these chilled for a refreshing snack with a zesty kick.

N.V.: Calories: 150, Fat: 8g, Carbs: 18g, Protein: 4g, Sugar: 10g

GINGER PECAN ENERGY BALLS

PREP: 15 min - **COOKING:** 0 min
MODE OF COOKING: No cook -
SERVES: 12
Ingr. list:
- 1 cup pecans
- 1 cup rolled oats
- 1/2 cup dried apricots, chopped
- 1/4 cup crystallized ginger, chopped
- 1/4 cup honey
- 1/2 tsp cinnamon
- Pinch of salt

Steps: In a food processor, pulse pecans and oats until finely ground. Add apricots, crystallized ginger, honey, cinnamon, and salt. Process the ingredients until they are thoroughly combined and the mixture holds together when pressed. Shape the mixture into balls, approximately 1 inch in diameter.

Recommendations: For an additional hint of spice, consider incorporating a pinch of nutmeg with the cinnamon. Keep the balls in an airtight container in the refrigerator for up to two weeks, or freeze them to extend their shelf life.

N.V.: Calories: 160, Fat: 9g, Carbs: 20g, Protein: 3g, Sugar: 12g

Chapter 11: Dessert Recipes

VEGAN CHOCOLATE AVOCADO CAKE

PREP: 20 min - **COOKING:** 30 min
MODE OF COOKING: Baking -
SERVES: 8

Ingr. list:
- 1 1/2 cups all-purpose flour
- 3/4 cup cocoa powder
- 1 tsp baking powder
- 1/2 tsp baking soda
- 1/4 tsp salt
- 2 ripe avocados, mashed
- 1 cup sugar
- 1 cup almond milk
- 1/3 cup coconut oil, melted
- 2 tsp vanilla extract

Steps: Preheat oven to 350°F (175°C). Prepare an 8-inch cake pan by greasing it and dusting it with flour. In a bowl, combine the flour, cocoa powder, baking powder, baking soda, and salt by whisking them together. In a separate bowl, mix the mashed avocados, sugar, almond milk, melted coconut oil, and vanilla extract until smooth. Slowly add the dry ingredients to the wet ingredients, stirring until just blended. Pour the batter into the prepared cake pan. Bake for 30 minutes, or until a toothpick inserted in the center comes out clean. Let the cake cool in the pan for 10 minutes before transferring it to a wire rack to cool completely.

Recommendations: Consider topping the cake with a vegan chocolate ganache or a light dusting of powdered sugar for a straightforward yet elegant finish. Enhance flavor by adding a shot of espresso to the batter to deepen the chocolate taste.

N.V.: Calories: 330, Fat: 15g, Carbs: 46g, Protein: 5g, Sugar: 25g

SPICED CARROT AND WALNUT PIE

PREP: 30 min - **COOKING:** 40 min
MODE OF COOKING: Baking -
SERVES: 8

Ingr. list:
- 2 cups grated carrots
- 1 cup chopped walnuts
- 1/2 cup raisins
- 1 vegan pie crust
- 3/4 cup almond milk
- 1/2 cup maple syrup
- 1/4 cup cornstarch
- 1 tsp cinnamon
- 1/2 tsp nutmeg
- 1/4 tsp cloves
- 1/4 tsp salt

Steps: Preheat oven to 375°F (190°C). Arrange the pie crust in a pie dish. In a saucepan set over medium heat, mix together carrots, almond milk, maple syrup, cornstarch, cinnamon, nutmeg, cloves, and salt. Cook until mixture thickens, about 10 min. Remove from heat and stir in walnuts and raisins. Pour filling into the pie crust. Bake for 40 min or until the filling is set and the crust is golden brown. Let cool before serving.

Recommendations: Serve with a dollop of vegan whipped cream or vanilla ice cream. Allow pie to cool completely to set properly before slicing.

N.V.: Calories: 310, Fat: 15g, Carbs: 42g, Protein: 4g, Sugar: 24g

LEMON BERRY POLENTA CAKE

PREP: 15 min - **COOKING:** 35 min
MODE OF COOKING: Baking -
SERVES: 10

Ingr. list:
- 1 1/2 cups fine polenta
- 1/2 cup almond flour
- 1 tsp baking powder
- 1/2 tsp salt
- 3/4 cup sugar
- 3/4 cup coconut oil, melted
- Juice and zest of 2 lemons
- 1 cup mixed berries (such as raspberries and blueberries)

Steps: Preheat oven to 350°F (175°C). Grease and flour a 9-inch round cake pan. In a bowl, mix polenta, almond flour, baking powder, and salt. In a separate bowl, whisk together sugar, melted coconut oil, lemon juice, and lemon zest until well combined. Gradually mix the dry ingredients into the wet ingredients until just combined. Gently fold in the mixed berries. Transfer the batter into the prepared cake pan and bake for 35 minutes, or until the cake is golden and a toothpick inserted into the center comes out clean. Allow the cake to cool in the pan for 10 minutes before moving it to a wire rack to cool completely.

Recommendations: This cake is best enjoyed fresh but can be stored in an airtight container for up to three days. Enhance with a light glaze made from lemon juice and powdered sugar if desired.

N.V.: Calories: 280, Fat: 16g, Carbs: 32g, Protein: 3g, Sugar: 18g

BLUEBERRY BANANA BREAD

PREP: 15 min - **COOKING:** 55 min
MODE OF COOKING: Baking -
SERVES: 8

Ingr. list:
- 3 ripe bananas, mashed
- 2 cups whole wheat flour
- 1/2 cup applesauce (unsweetened)
- 3/4 cup organic sugar
- 1/2 cup fresh blueberries
- 1 tsp baking soda
- 1/2 tsp salt
- 1 tsp vanilla extract

Steps: Preheat oven to 350°F (175°C). Grease and flour a 9x5-inch loaf pan. In a large bowl, mix together mashed bananas, applesauce, and sugar. Add vanilla extract and stir until combined. In a separate bowl, whisk together flour, baking soda, and salt. Gradually add the dry ingredients to the wet ingredients, mixing until just combined to avoid overmixing. Gently fold in the blueberries. Transfer the batter into the prepared loaf pan and bake for 55 minutes, or until a toothpick inserted into the center comes out clean. Allow the bread to cool in the pan for 10 minutes before turning it out onto a wire rack to cool completely.

Recommendations: Utilize very ripe bananas for the best flavor. Be careful not to overmix the batter to ensure the bread remains tender. Sprinkle a little raw sugar on top before baking for a crunchy crust.

N.V.: Calories: 210, Fat: 0.5g, Carbs: 48g, Protein: 4g, Sugar: 25g

RUSTIC PEACH AND CHIA TART

PREP: 20 min - **COOKING:** 25 min
MODE OF COOKING: Baking -
SERVES: 8

Ingr. list:
- 1 1/2 cups spelt flour
- 1/2 cup coconut oil, solid
- 1/4 cup ice water
- 3 large peaches, sliced
- 2 Tbsp chia seeds
- 1/4 cup maple syrup
- 1 tsp cinnamon
- Pinch of salt

Steps: Preheat oven to 375°F (190°C). In a mixing bowl, mix spelt flour and salt together. Cut in coconut oil until the mixture looks like coarse crumbs. Slowly add ice water, stirring until a dough forms. Roll out the dough on a floured surface and place it into a 9-inch tart pan. Arrange peach slices on the crust, sprinkle with chia seeds, and drizzle with maple syrup. Lightly dust with cinnamon. Bake at 350 degrees Fahrenheit for 25 minutes, or until the crust turns golden and the peaches are tender. Allow the tart to cool before serving.

Recommendations: Enhance the serving with a dollop of coconut whipped cream or a scoop of vegan vanilla ice cream for added indulgence. Use a combination of peaches and nectarines for a more complex flavor.

N.V.: Calories: 240, Fat: 12g, Carbs: 32g, Protein: 3g, Sugar: 12g

VEGAN PUMPKIN CHEESECAKE

PREP: 30 min - **COOKING:** 60 min
MODE OF COOKING: Baking -
SERVES: 10

Ingr. list:
- 1 1/2 cups raw cashews, soaked overnight
- 1 cup pumpkin puree
- 1/2 cup coconut cream
- 3/4 cup maple syrup
- 1/4 cup cornstarch
- 2 tsp pumpkin pie spice
- 1 cup almond flour
- 1/2 cup rolled oats
- 1/4 cup coconut oil, melted
- 1 tsp vanilla extract
- Pinch of salt

Steps: Preheat oven to 350°F (175°C). For the crust, combine almond flour, rolled oats, melted coconut oil, and a pinch of salt in a food processor. Process until a sticky mixture forms. Press into the bottom of a 9-inch springform pan. For the filling, blend soaked cashews, pumpkin puree, coconut cream, maple syrup, cornstarch, pumpkin pie spice, and vanilla extract until smooth and creamy. Pour the filling over the crust and smooth out the top. Bake for 60 minutes or until the edges are firm but the center remains slightly jiggly. Allow it to cool to room temperature, then chill in the refrigerator for at least 4 hours, or preferably overnight.

Recommendations: Decorate with a sprinkle of cinnamon or chopped pecans before serving. Ensure the cheesecake is completely cooled before chilling to prevent cracks.

N.V.: Calories: 350, Fat: 22g, Carbs: 34g, Protein: 6g, Sugar: 20g

OATMEAL BANANA BREAKFAST COOKIES

PREP: 10 min - **COOKING:** 15 min
MODE OF COOKING: Baking -
SERVES: 12

Ingr. list:
- 2 ripe bananas, mashed
- 1 cup rolled oats
- 1/4 cup almond butter
- 1/4 cup unsweetened shredded coconut
- 1/4 cup dried cranberries
- 1 tsp vanilla extract
- 1/2 tsp cinnamon
- Pinch of salt

Steps: Preheat oven to 350°F (175°C). Place parchment paper on a baking sheet. In a large bowl, mix together mashed bananas, oats, almond butter, shredded coconut, dried cranberries, vanilla extract, cinnamon, and a pinch of salt. Scoop tablespoonfuls of the mixture onto the baking sheet and press each lightly to form a cookie shape. Bake for 15 minutes, or until the edges turn golden brown.

Recommendations: Keep the cookies in an airtight container for up to a week, or freeze them for extended storage. These cookies are perfect for a quick breakfast or a nutritious snack when you're on the move.
N.V.: Calories: 98, Fat: 4.5g, Carbs: 13g, Protein: 2g, Sugar: 5g

ALMOND AND DATE ENERGY BARS

PREP: 20 min - **COOKING:** 0 min
MODE OF COOKING: No cook -
SERVES: 10

Ingr. list:
- 1 cup raw almonds
- 1 cup pitted dates
- 1/4 cup flaxseeds
- 1/4 cup unsweetened cocoa powder
- 1/4 cup almond butter
- 1 tsp vanilla extract
- Pinch of salt

Steps: In a food processor, combine almonds, dates, flaxseeds, cocoa powder, and salt. Process until mixture is finely chopped and sticks together. Mix in almond butter and vanilla extract, then process the ingredients again until they come together into a sticky dough. Firmly press the dough into an 8x8 inch baking pan that has been lined. Place the pan in the refrigerator and chill for at least one hour before cutting the dough into bars.

Recommendations: Wrap bars individually for a convenient, grab-and-go snack. For a smoother texture, soak dates in warm water for 10 minutes before processing.
N.V.: Calories: 200, Fat: 11g, Carbs: 23g, Protein: 5g, Sugar: 15g

PUMPKIN SPICE QUINOA BARS

PREP: 15 min - **COOKING:** 25 min
MODE OF COOKING: Baking -
SERVES: 12

Ingr. list:
- 1 cup quinoa, cooked and cooled
- 1/2 cup pumpkin puree
- 1/4 cup maple syrup
- 1/4 cup chopped pecans
- 1/4 cup dried cranberries
- 1/4 cup almond flour
- 2 tsp pumpkin pie spice
- 1 tsp vanilla extract
- 1/4 tsp salt

Steps: Preheat oven to 375°F (190°C). Line an 8x8 inch baking pan with parchment paper. In a large bowl, thoroughly combine all the ingredients. Transfer the mixture to the prepared pan, pressing it down firmly. Bake for 25 minutes, or until the edges turn golden brown and the center is firm. Allow the bars to cool completely in the pan before slicing them.

Recommendations: To maintain freshness and firmness, store the bars in the refrigerator. Sprinkle a few extra pecans or a light drizzle of additional maple syrup on top before baking for extra flavor and crunch.

N.V.: Calories: 140, Fat: 5g, Carbs: 20g, Protein: 3g, Sugar: 10g

COCONUT CHIA SEED BARS

PREP: 15 min - **COOKING:** 0 min
MODE OF COOKING: Refrigeration -
SERVES: 12

Ingr. list:
- 1 cup chia seeds
- 1 cup coconut flakes, unsweetened
- 1/2 cup almond butter
- 1/2 cup maple syrup
- 1/2 cup dried cherries, chopped
- 1/4 cup almond milk
- 1 tsp vanilla extract
- Pinch of salt

Steps: In a large bowl, mix together chia seeds, coconut flakes, almond butter, maple syrup, dried cherries, almond milk, vanilla extract, and salt until well combined. Firmly press the mixture into an 8x8 inch baking dish lined with parchment paper. Refrigerate for at least 4 hours, or overnight, to allow the mixture to firm up. Once set, cut into bars and serve.

Recommendations: Store the bars in an airtight container in the refrigerator to keep them fresh. For a chocolate twist, melt dark chocolate and drizzle over the bars before chilling.

N.V.: Calories: 230, Fat: 14g, Carbs: 24g, Protein: 5g, Sugar: 12g

LEMON POPPY SEED PROTEIN BARS

PREP: 20 min - **COOKING:** 0 min
MODE OF COOKING: Refrigeration -
SERVES: 10

Ingr. list:
- 1 cup rolled oats
- 1/2 cup protein powder, plant-based
- 1/4 cup poppy seeds
- 1/4 cup honey (or agave for vegan option)
- 1/4 cup coconut oil, melted
- Zest and juice of 1 lemon
- Pinch of salt

Steps: In a mixing bowl, combine rolled oats, protein powder, poppy seeds, lemon zest, and salt. Whisk together honey, coconut oil, and lemon juice in a separate bowl until smooth. Pour the wet ingredients into the dry ingredients and mix until they are thoroughly combined. Press the mixture evenly into an 8x8 inch baking dish that has been lined with parchment paper. Refrigerate the mixture for at least 3 hours, or until it is firmly set. Once set, cut into bars and serve.

Recommendations: For added texture, include crushed almonds or walnuts in the mix. Keep the bars stored in the refrigerator to ensure they remain firm and fresh.

N.V.: Calories: 180, Fat: 9g, Carbs: 20g, Protein: 7g, Sugar: 10g

MANGO AND PASSION FRUIT SORBET

PREP: 20 min - **COOKING:** 0 min
MODE OF COOKING: Freezing -
SERVES: 6
Ingr. list:
- 2 ripe mangoes, peeled and cubed
- 1 cup passion fruit pulp
- 1/2 cup water
- 1/4 cup maple syrup
- Juice of 1 lime

Steps: Blend mangoes, passion fruit pulp, water, maple syrup, and lime juice in a blender until smooth. Pour the mixture into an ice cream maker and churn according to the manufacturer's instructions until it reaches a sorbet consistency. Transfer the sorbet to a freezer-safe container and freeze until firm, about 2 hours.

Recommendations: If you do not have an ice cream maker, pour the mixture into a shallow pan and freeze, stirring every 30 minutes to break up ice crystals. Serve with a sprinkle of toasted coconut flakes for added texture.

N.V.: Calories: 110, Fat: 0.3g, Carbs: 28g, Protein: 1g, Sugar: 25g

PEACH AND RASPBERRY CRISP

PREP: 15 min - **COOKING:** 45 min
MODE OF COOKING: Baking -
SERVES: 8

Ingr. list:
- 4 cups fresh peaches, sliced
- 2 cups fresh raspberries
- 1/2 cup rolled oats
- 1/2 cup almond flour
- 1/4 cup chopped almonds
- 1/4 cup maple syrup
- 1/4 cup coconut oil, melted
- 1 tsp cinnamon
- Pinch of salt

Steps: Preheat oven to 375°F (190°C). In a large bowl, toss peaches and raspberries with 2 tablespoons of maple syrup and pour into a greased baking dish. In another bowl, mix rolled oats, almond flour, chopped almonds, remaining maple syrup, melted coconut oil, cinnamon, and salt until crumbly. Sprinkle the oat mixture evenly over the fruit. Bake for 45 minutes or until the topping is golden brown and the fruit is bubbly.

Recommendations: Serve warm with a scoop of vegan vanilla ice cream or coconut whipped cream. For added crunch, include a handful of pumpkin seeds in the topping mixture.

N.V.: Calories: 220, Fat: 10g, Carbs: 32g, Protein: 4g, Sugar: 19g

WATERMELON MINT GRANITA

PREP: 15 min - **COOKING:** 3 hr
MODE OF COOKING: Freezing -
SERVES: 8
Ingr. list:
- 4 cups watermelon, seeded and cubed
- 1/4 cup fresh mint leaves
- 1/4 cup lime juice

- 1/4 cup agave syrup

Steps: Puree watermelon, mint leaves, lime juice, and agave syrup in a blender until smooth. Pour the mixture into a shallow baking dish and place in the freezer. Every 30 minutes for about 3 hours, scrape the mixture with a fork to create flaky, icy crystals. Serve the granita in chilled bowls or glasses.

Recommendations: Add a splash of sparkling water to each serving for a refreshing, fizzy twist. Garnish with extra mint leaves and lime slices for a festive presentation.

N.V.: Calories: 70, Fat: 0g, Carbs: 18g, Protein: 1g, Sugar: 16g

STRAWBERRY BASIL SORBET

PREP: 15 min - **COOKING:** 0 min
MODE OF COOKING: Freezing -
SERVES: 6

Ingr. list:
- 4 cups fresh strawberries, hulled
- 1/4 cup fresh basil leaves
- 1/3 cup agave syrup
- 1 tbsp lemon juice

Steps: Blend strawberries, basil leaves, agave syrup, and lemon juice until smooth in a blender. Pour the mixture into an ice cream maker and churn according to the manufacturer's instructions until it reaches a sorbet consistency. Transfer the sorbet to a freezer-safe container and freeze until firm, about 2 hours.

Recommendations: For a more intense basil flavor, infuse the agave syrup with extra basil leaves before blending. Garnish with additional fresh basil leaves or strawberry slices when serving.

N.V.: Calories: 90, Fat: 0.2g, Carbs: 23g, Protein: 1g, Sugar: 21g

KIWI LIME PIE

PREP: 20 min - **COOKING:** 0 min
MODE OF COOKING: Chilling -
SERVES: 8

Ingr. list:
- 1 1/2 cups raw cashews, soaked for 4 hours and drained
- 1 cup fresh kiwi, peeled and sliced
- 1/2 cup coconut cream
- 1/4 cup lime juice
- 1/4 cup agave syrup
- 1 cup dates, pitted
- 1 cup raw almonds
- 1 tsp lime zest
- Pinch of salt

Steps: For the crust, process dates and almonds in a food processor until a sticky dough forms. Press the mixture into the bottom of a greased 9-inch pie dish. Blend cashews, kiwi slices, coconut cream, lime juice, agave syrup, and salt until smooth and creamy for the filling. Pour the filling over the crust and smooth the top with a spatula. Chill in the refrigerator for at least 4 hours, or until set. Garnish with lime zest and additional kiwi slices before serving.

Recommendations: Freeze the pie for 1 hour before serving for a firmer texture. Drizzle with a light honey-lime syrup for added sweetness if desired.

N.V.: Calories: 310, Fat: 18g, Carbs: 34g, Protein: 6g, Sugar: 23g

BLACKBERRY APPLE CRUMBLE

PREP: 15 min - **COOKING:** 45 min
MODE OF COOKING: Baking -
SERVES: 6

Ingr. list:
- 3 cups fresh blackberries
- 2 apples, peeled, cored, and sliced
- 1/2 cup rolled oats
- 1/2 cup almond meal
- 1/4 cup coconut oil, melted
- 1/3 cup maple syrup
- 1 tsp cinnamon
- Pinch of nutmeg

Steps: Preheat oven to 350°F (175°C). Mix blackberries and apples with 1/3 of the maple syrup and pour into a baking dish. In a bowl, combine oats, almond meal, cinnamon, nutmeg, and melted coconut oil. Mix until crumbly. Sprinkle the crumble mixture evenly over the fruit. Bake for 45 minutes or until the topping is golden brown and the fruits are bubbling.

Recommendations: Serve warm with a scoop of vegan vanilla ice cream or coconut whipped cream. Add a touch of lemon zest to the fruit mixture for an extra zing.

N.V.: Calories: 290, Fat: 15g, Carbs: 37g, Protein: 4g, Sugar: 25g

3-Week Meal Plan

Week 1

DAY	BREAKFAST	LUNCH	DINNER	SNACK	DESSERT
Monday	Tropical Green Energy Smoothie	Crunchy Kale and Apple Salad	Eggplant and Chickpea Bake	Roasted Red Pepper Hummus	
Tuesday	Berry Oat Smoothie Bowl	Mediterranean Quinoa Salad	Sweet Potato and Black Bean Casserole		Lemon Berry Polenta Cake
Wednesday	Spiced Pumpkin Smoothie	Spicy Lentil and Sweet Potato Salad	Mushroom and Kale Strata	Baked Zucchini Fries	
Thursday	Avocado Citrus Smoothie	Roasted Beet and Goat Cheese Salad	Spinach and Mushroom Lasagna	Spicy Black Bean and Corn Dip	
Friday	Golden Turmeric Smoothie Bowl	Spicy Tomato and Lentil Soup	Ratatouille Baked Ziti		Vegan Chocolate Avocado Cake
Saturday	Minty Melon Smoothie	Creamy Broccoli and Almond Soup	Sweet Potato Shepherd's Pie	Crispy Kale Chips	
Sunday	Almond Oat Banana Pancakes	Moroccan Sweet Potato and Chickpea Stew	Thai Tempeh and Basil Stir-Fry		Blueberry Banana Bread

DAY	BREAKFAST	LUNCH	DINNER	SNACK	DESSERT
Monday	Zucchini Oat Waffles	Asian Pear and Arugula Salad	Szechuan Eggplant and Mushroom Stir-Fry		Rustic Peach and Chia Tart
Tuesday	Blueberry Lemon Pancakes	Avocado and Black Bean Salad	Lemongrass Tempeh Stir-Fry	Parmesan Cauliflower Poppers	
Wednesday	Cinnamon Buckwheat Pancakes	Hearty Mushroom Barley Soup	Red Lentil and Spinach Curry		Pumpkin Spice Quinoa Bars
Thursday	Chocolate Chip Oatmeal Waffles	Spicy Thai Tempeh Wrap	Moroccan Quinoa and Chickpea Bowl	Herbed Yogurt and Cucumber Dip	
Friday	Savory Quinoa and Kale Breakfast Bowl	Mediterranean Chickpea Salad Sandwich	Spicy Broccoli and Peanut Stir-Fry		Mango and Passion Fruit Sorbet
Saturday	Tempeh Scramble Taco Bowl	Avocado and Hummus Veggie Wrap	Asian Brown Rice and Edamame Bowl	Almond and Chia Energy Bites	
Sunday	Sweet Potato and Black Bean Breakfast Hash	Grilled Portobello Mushroom Sandwich	Mediterranean Farro and Chickpea Bowl		Strawberry Basil Sorbet

DAY	BREAKFAST	LUNCH	DINNER	SNACK	DESSERT
Monday	Mushroom and Spinach Breakfast Bowl	Roasted Vegetable and Pesto Panini	Curried Lentil and Wild Rice Bowl	Cocoa and Walnut Energy Bites	
Tuesday	Pear and Almond Overnight Oats	Curried Chickpea Wrap	Sweet Potato and Black Bean Burrito Bowl		Kiwi Lime Pie
Wednesday	Avocado Toast with Radish and Arugula	Butternut Squash and Red Lentil Stew	Roasted Vegetable and Barley Bowl	Matcha Green Tea Energy Balls	
Thursday	Pear and Almond Overnight Oats	Curried Chickpea Wrap	Curried Lentil and Wild Rice Bowl		Vegan Pumpkin Cheesecake
Friday	Golden Turmeric Smoothie Bowl	Creamy Broccoli and Almond Soup	Lemongrass Tempeh Stir-Fry	Peach and Raspberry Crisp	
Saturday	Minty Melon Smoothie	Spicy Tomato and Lentil Soup	Ratatouille Baked Ziti	Coconut Chia Seed Bars	
Sunday	Almond Oat Banana Pancakes	Crunchy Kale and Apple Salad	Coconut Curry Medley		Peach and Raspberry Crisp

Made in the USA
Las Vegas, NV
23 November 2024

12505710R00070